the
MIST
of
YESTERDAY

the MIST *of* YESTERDAY

POEMS OF
HOPE AND COMFORT IN A
TROUBLED WORLD

COLIN PRITCHARD

The Mist of Yesterday

Copyright © 2024 Colin J Pritchard.

No part of this book shall be reproduced or transmitted in any form or by any means, electronic or mechanical, including photocopying, recording, or by any information retrieval system without written permission from the publisher.

ISBN 9798872477679

A Faithful Friend

The poems I have written come from the heart
although the mind plays a part;
emotions too come into play
with all I see day by day,

And yet there is one thing that must be read;
something important when all else is said
which stands above much that is clear
and is one thing that we hold so dear.

We are all human and prone to fail
but one thing is certain to never pale,
and that is to be faithful in all that we do,
for there are many others like me and like you,

Who feel so discouraged, and prone to fall,
we can help them to see there is One for us all,
our Creator and Saviour who will not let us down
who died on a cross to give us a crown.

There is no one so faithful as this dearest Friend
who will love us and help us right to the end.
His name is Jesus, take hold of His hand
He never will leave you; will teach you to stand;

Until when at last this short life you will leave,
if you have trusted Him then you will not grieve,
His faithfulness carries you to Heaven above
safe and secure in His arms of love.

The Mist of Yesterday

I opened my eyes and looked around
My feet were resting on solid ground
or so I thought when senses came
things around here were not the same.

What is that I see? The walls are bare.
Table here and bed over there.
Am I awake? Is this a dream?
I'm not so sure, what does it seem.

A tear falls down, where am I now?
Inside I feel my heart does bow.
The pain I feel, from whence it comes,
and why is it there? Confusion reigns.

Will no one help? Where have they gone?
The loneliness. Is this my judge?
Did I do this? What have I done?
All men have left me, all alone.

It is inside where none can see
I scream I cry, don't pity me.
The guilt I feel, has long since past
but I am left alone at last.

Others see the outside pain
I, alone the inner feel
private feelings, silent thoughts,
does all this life just come to nought?

I once was wed and loved a wife
I hurt and damaged, like a knife.
Our love was good and pure and clean
but something came so false and mean.

What of the future? Can there be hope?
Where is my God and promise sure.
He alone can lift from dust
In him alone I put my trust.

The Mist of Yesterday

He can make the hardest soft
and lift us again to heights aloft.
Man alone will always fail
but he can evermore prevail.

Please stay with me friend and God
I cling to you and hold your cross.
Hold me tight and lift from sod
Til other all I count not loss.

Only you above all else
Let me see your holy face.
That look, so full of gentleness,
of mercy and of endless grace.

Forgiveness, now but those I hurt
Bring healing balm and free from pain.
The things you show me, words you taught
please give to them and cover shame.

I ask for nothing else but this
restore, forgive and give your love
to all I love with humble heart
and change me, make me from above.

What is a Friend

What is a friend but one who feels
Who knows and thinks and loves at last
When all around have long since gone.
When mist and mire have held me fast.

They do not judge but know the end
of love's unbounding, giving frame.
Tireless, unswerving, they will send
themselves and never once to blame.

The dirt and dust they do ignore
and see beyond what others see
the inner strength and life, though poor
their longing is to see me free.

What would I do without you, friend?
My life it would be lost and mean
If you weren't there and will to bend
and lift me with your hand so clean.

Please don't leave me or I'd die
but that is not the thing you do
your heart, it feels and shares the cry,
I know you love me, through and through.

Silence

The whisper, can you hear it now?
So gentle, warm and friendly too.
Not all can hear it's simple tone.
Silence alone is all they knew.

You will be changed if you allow
that whisper to penetrate your brow.
Listen, listen and it will speak
to give you strength when you are weak.

Draw aside from this world's strife
This inner voice will give new life.
Some do not want this inner peace
they want the fighting not to cease.

Security is in the toil
of bustling, straining urgent way
but when the secret warmth is found
it brings a bright new quiet day.

War

They fight without and fight within
Struggle, strife and angry look
to harm and hurt, they are akin
and count the cost of which they took.
It's taking, taking, taking more
satisfaction is far from here
Selfishness and private war
Stealing all that we hold dear.
The strain apparent upon the face
Body bends and cannot take
the force inflicted without grace
Illness, pain, this will it make.
Give up, give up, not worth the cost
it ends in death and life is lost.
Not just to those but all around
where grace and mercy is not found.

The Storm

The storm, it rages on the sea
of life. It's there for all mankind.
How handled, it can set us free
Examine it, there's much to find.

The reason that it comes and goes
is often missed and seen as pain.
It brings the sighs and feels the woes
but can bring blessing and a gain.

It changes and disturbs the nest
and makes us feel so insecure.
Allow it and it gives the best
healing us and makes us pure.

Aggression

Why do we fight with toil and strife?
Why is there no meaning to this life?
Why do we not see the end in it all?
To fight and struggle and then to fall.

We dominate others and tread them all down,
walk on them, threaten them, give them a frown.
To what is it's purpose, what is the cost?
Why do we do it? When we are all lost.

We have to be king and prove it to all
forgetting that one day we will not stand tall.
One day we will topple and fall to the ground
No more aggression, not even a sound.

LOVE

Who can fathom what love is
Who knows from where it has come
Can we see it and know it
Is it only reserved for some?

Love is for all and comes without cost
Love is for you and all who are lost.
The price has been paid and we can receive
the love that is offered, so we can live.

WHY?

I often ask 'why?' There is no reply
no answer to satisfy you and I.
Why is this so? What reason is this?
I only get silence. Is there something I miss?

In silence is reason enough for us all.
It is in life, until we are called
Only then will we know the reason and why
and then understand the tears that are dry.

BEING CLOSE

I must feel you be close to me.
The reason to live and feel to be free.
If you turn away I surely must cry
The reason is gone and then I must die.

Stay close by my side and we will go on.
Come whatever may be, I rely upon
your presence with me and near by my side
it humbles me, washes me, deals with my pride.

The Heart

The heart is an anchor and strength to the soul
The seat of emotion, and with it we're whole
Guard it and keep it and hold it so close
It can be deception, with pride and a boast.

Out of it stems all the issues of life
There is a cost if used full of strife
Allow it to change us and prove that can be
a heart full of gentleness, our eyes we will see.

Isolation

Don't push me away. What have I done?
Shut me in prison and shut out the sun.
If not in this world, then where can I go?
I'm frightened and lonely, becoming so slow.

I shuffle along and life is not there
I look for it, long for it, wondering where
to go from here now. What do I do?
To satisfy others, do I have to prove?

The world does not want me and turns me away
to another direction. I come to pray
for mercy and grace from my Father above
The Father so full of goodness and love.

He's been here and knows what it's like, I am sure
He suffered and gave and lived for the poor.
The world did not want him and cast him aside
Not for his own wrong was the reason he died.

We suffer alone for the wrong that we do
but he was alone and that much he knew.
So therefore he comes and walks by my side
and does not condemn me, if I walk not in pride.

LONELINESS

So many are lonely but what will you do?
How will you help them to make them anew?
Can we but blame them and cast them aside
and judge them alone as we walk by in pride.

They're hurting and bleeding and damaged inside
where no one can see for there they do hide
The struggles within are not like without
they're much more so private and alone, there's no doubt.

We must see beyond the outside and within
and try to understand and not just see the sin
but look deep inside as Jesus would have done
and open up the heart and let in the sun.

GIVING

How much do I give and what motive is there?
What reason to love? What reason to share?
Is it for what I can but receive?
For something I get to help me to live?

Please help me to give and not to want back
Giving again and nothing to slack
My reward is within and I have not lost
for others to gain, I count not the cost.

My brother, my sister my family too
are ever enriched and have something new
When I give to them and sacrifice done
within myself I know that I have just won.

The Light

The light, it shines brightly and penetrates the soul
Allow it to illumine and light up the whole
It will be your friend if you want it to be
Will change you and make you and let you be free.

It's sometimes so painful and comes with a cost
but when it is done it saves what was lost
Not only does this, but much more besides
It gives you abundantly and dressed like a bride.

It purifies, cleanses and makes you feel new.
Your head lifted up, your words no more few
are filled with new life and new hope for the lost
Those that have fallen at very great cost.

With others set free from the prison they're in
Those with heads bowed and conscious of sin
Many are they who fail and who fall
Lift up their heads when they hear the call.

The call that they hear will give hope for them now
All it will take is for their heads to bow
under the light that will set them so free
Given by one who died on a tree.

Guilt

'Guilty', 'guilty', the cry will go out,
of that I can promise, of that there's no doubt.

With head hung in shame, the prisoner begs more,
for mercy and kindness, for that he implores.

The crowd they do roar and bay for his blood,
they cry out 'away' in terrible mood.

The Mist of Yesterday

Straining and swaying with hatred inside,
they pick up the stones and wish he had died.

But what do I hear, as trembling, I see,
another who comes and with kindness, says he;

'Put down your stones now and let this man go,
I see in his heart and this thing I know.

The punishment lay it upon my own head,
I'll take his place until I lay dead.

But set this one free and let him now live,
the ultimate sacrifice, this is what I give.

The crowd they did roar and cry out in rage,
that one now should dare to rattle their cage.

But judge said 'enough, let this thing be done,
it's wholly permissible, take now this Son,

And do him the deed that he has pursued
and he shall now suffer the shame and the rude.'

The prisoner set free and as standing alone,
his death sentence now passed from him to this one,

who cruelly treated and left there to die,
had taken his place and he did not know why.

The tears now falling great drops to the ground,
the words now lay silent, they could not be found.

He fell to his knees and cried out to God,
why did this stranger, along his path he trod.

In the distance he heard the great cries of the mob
this man who had come, none other than God

As they tore him apart, this stranger so kind
now the prisoner set free, in body and mind.

Children

They sing, they play, they laugh and shout
They do not care who is about
So full of fun and happiness
So much to give, so much to bless.

The years go by so quickly away
Gone is the time that children can play
We long and we pine for the years have gone by
The innocence of youth, where does it fly?

As adults we grow and now know so much
about life and it's trials and stressing to touch
Our minds drift back and the past without care
Where is our childhood, please tell us where?

So much we must leave as something before
we value its lessons but like waves on the shore
The tide will go out and leave us alone
with memories of children, of which we were one.

Old Age

With hair all white and wrinkled skin,
no one knows the pain we're in.
We hobble here, we hobble there
and body shows signs of wear and tear.

Our minds go back to long ago
The people we knew, the places to show
to others who will come behind
impart our knowledge from our mind.

We have so much to give to those we love
So much to enrich their lives and prove
that old age can at last lay down
satisfied that it leaves a crown.

THE SEA

The sea gives life but also death
and takes away our very breath
but it can also show us how
to harness the destructive power.

We all have just that kind of choice
for good or evil have a voice
The power we have the power to choose
destructive power or like a cruise

That floats upon the storm tossed sea
brings calm and peace to you and me
and helps us to live with peace of mind
instead of the destructive kind.

THE MIND

The mind is set but the body sleeps
or does it? As the mind keeps
control of the body and so
the body acts but the mind says 'no'.

The battle goes on and rages long
into the night but my mind is a song
I toss and turn and run to and fro
in my dreams which are short and soon come and go.

Confusion reigns and tiredness abounds
What is this life where my mind, full of sounds
never goes to sleep. Does it never cease?
My body needs rest but 1 need my peace.

The Mask

Who are you? From where do you come?
What do I see? What is this strange thing?
In front of your face, covering you some
maybe not real, or maybe a dream.

I feel insecure and wondering now
should I be frightened and take to my heels?
No, it's only a mask does everyone show
how do you think and how do you feel?

The mask may be gentle, the mask may be kind
The mask is not real and covers the mind
The mask brings confusion, respectable too
There's many for sale, for me and for you.

Blindness

Open your eyes but you cannot see
the flowers around, the birds and the trees.
The sun and the sky, the raindrop so fine
taken for granted the things that do shine.

Some open their eyes but they cannot see
the things all around for you and for me
Beautiful, precious things hidden from view
only exposed to some of the few.

Some don't see the beautiful things
Tiny ant or butterflies wings
So busy rushing and racing around
Making their money, with their eyes on the ground.

SADNESS

Do not be sad but look all around
Look at the sky and look at the ground
Look at your body, your soul and your mind
See those around you who try to be kind.

The positive things can always be seen
Don't look at the negative, nasty and mean
The critical, callous when smiling is bad
the things that you could have or things that you had.

Look up and not down when things are so hard
When life and your health has dealt a wrong card
Your spirit and soul will soar up on wings
Your mind has a song, encouraged to sing.

ENVY

Why do you envy the man with the wealth
With fast car, large house and bursting with health?
The money accrued gives holiday fine
Do we ask, why isn't this mine?

All men are different and backgrounds too
Their wealth and fame for many or few
Why look on the outside, when different within
One day it will crumble, real wealth will be seen.

Our minds can be filled with jewels and gold
Enriching us whether we're young or we're old
Deep down inside us the real gold dwells
That is the story that all of us tell.

Greed

The old man struggled and hobbled along
Slow now, his strength and warmth was gone
He fumbled and fumbled to get out a coin
The crowd standing round, their patience was gone.

At last he had found it and gave to the shop
nervously glancing as around him they stopped
The shopkeeper smiled and gave him his change
Why was he crying and feeling so strange?

He took now his shopping and stumbled without
Why is it like this? Of that there's no doubt
we all come to that place like the elderly one
and many around like to shut out the sun.

Illness

She lay in the bed, the minutes rushed by
Why oh why, will no one say why?
Once I was young and fit, full of life
now I am cut to the heart like a knife

Others were kind and saw to her need
washing her carefully, giving her feed
No one could see the small tear that she shed
there in the quiet as she lay on her bed.

Dying

Why am I frightened, what's this about?
Why are they rushing and some seem to shout?
Please won't you tell me? Why do I feel
so strange now, and why do I not want my meal?

My appetite's gone, my heart it does race
Why do I sweat and perspire on my face?
Please, please stop rushing and just hold my hand
I feel I am going to another land.

What do I see, and what do I hear?
The singing around me, the brightness
I feared I think I see Jesus with arms open wide
and eyes full of love, as for me he died.

Don't bring me back, I want to go now
Yes, I can see him the beauty, somehow
The fear has all gone, the light now has dawned
I will awake on some other morn.

The Quiet Place

Why do you rush so, and busy around
It's gathering dust all over the ground
So much to do and so much to see
So very busy for you and for me.

We need work to live, you busily tell
Why do you shout and why do you yell?
There's so much ado about nothing I fear
Why do I long to be out of here?

I go' to my room and shut to the door
I fall on the bed and roll on the floor
Trying to shut out the busiest life
by holding my ears and heart full of strife.

At last I am still and lay all alone
This is the place for which I have longed
The place that is quiet and so very still
My mind so relaxed and starting to fill

with thoughts of afar so, pleasant and grand
I shut tight my eyes and open my hand
And grasp what I see and take it to heart
This is my comfort and this is my part.

War

Why do you fight so and why do you war?
Why do you hurt and rage and do roar?
What is the reason? Why is it so?
Where is the giving and where does it go?

Fighting will take and hurt us as well
gritting the teeth and feeling like hell.
Give it all up and live like a king
Your heart is alive, your body will sing.

Peace

The stream runs down the mountainside
nowhere to go, nowhere to hide
over the hills and over the stones
rippling, moving, this is my home.

Gentleness, gentleness, smooth rocks it makes
Hearing it, seeing it, out to the lakes.
Constantly pouring and never to cease
Here's where I sit and here I find peace.

Alone

All alone, yet not alone, what a thing is this?
Here is where I find my rest. This is where is bliss.
Someone else is here beside me, though you cannot see
in the mind and in the heart and in the secret me.

He never leaves me, always here and talks within my soul
Without him, I would never be a person now made whole.
Only I can see him and hear his lovely voice
He calms me, loves me, comforts, and leaves me with a choice.

He never forces, oh so gentle, always waiting here
And when I choose to go away and walk the path of fear
Still awaits me, longs to hear me turn upon the door
He takes away my foolish wandering, rich instead of poor.

The Universe

Lift up your eyes and look to the stars
Saturn, Jupiter, Uranus and Mars.
See them all there as faithful each night
they shine with a dazzling brilliance of light.

See the great sun and the moon shines at night
One is so brilliant and one not so bright
But no matter how big or how small they are
they're bigger than we are and brighter by far.

When we look up and gaze in the sky
it lifts up our hearts and forget to ask 'why'
It takes off our minds from the troubles we're in
and stops us from searching and looking for sin.

It helps us to know there is someone above
with arms open wide and a heart full of love
For us he's alive and he'll always be there
Just surely as for men the universe is shared.

Welcome

Welcome, stranger, come right in
sit here, no matter what state you are in.
My home is your home and you are my guest
whether you are at your poorest or best.

Don't be afraid, you are welcome here
I bring you peace, just give me your fear.
Sit and enjoy the treasures around
make yourself comfortable, not on the ground.

You used to be kicked and spat on I know
as with begging bowl you bowed down so low
but now you have peace and all that I own
is shared now for you including my throne.

Searching

For whom do you live, for what do you seek?
Why are you searching? Why do you not speak?
Endlessly looking and wanting for more
Nothing to say, with eyes on the floor.

Is it for more, you are wanting, my friend?
Is what you want, that I can lend?
No, this is not for that you will seek
For why you are searching and why you don't speak.

Pictures

Look at the picture. What do you see?
Different for you and different for me?
All see things differently when they do view
A picture is different for me and for you.

No one is wrong and no one is right
When you look at a picture, no need to fight
Accept one another and differing views
No matter by one or many or few.

Home

Where is home? What is it like?
Is it bricks and mortar, or is it on your bike?
Is it in your car or under a bridge?
Or in a doorway or on a bench?

Is home a bundle of dirty rags
or wrapped up in filthy carrier bags?
Perhaps it lies in a mansion bright
or under the stars in the dead of night.

What is your home? Where do you belong?
With a family of love or a house of wrong?
Look into your heart and you will find,
your home, where there is peace of mind.

Daddy

Where are you Daddy? I stumble along
hurting my feet and my heart with no song.
The brambles, they cut me and tear my hands raw
my knees, they are bleeding and ever so sore.

Please tell me Daddy, I'm all alone here
trembling and frightened and shedding a tear.
The darkness around me fills me with grief
others have left me and think I'm a thief.

My clothes are in tatters, they are what I can find,
when I steal from the dustbins, then know they are mine.
At least I am warmer and sheltered from wind
when I'm wearing these rags, in the state I am in.

Daddy, my Daddy, if you were just here,
you'd hug we and warm me and take away fear.
I'd hold you so close and never let go
just in my mind I can see you and that's all I know.

MOTHER

As I think back and enter my dreams
think of my Mother and somehow it seems
that she is so real and she I can touch
although she has long gone I miss her so much.

There is so much pain, to her I would run
She would open her arms and welcome her son.
Her hug then would tell me that everything's well
I'd feel it was Heaven, instead of in hell.

Oh Mother, my heart aches and longs for your voice,
comforting, soothing, gentle and soft.
With tears in my eyes, your memory gives hope
and gives me encouragement and ability to cope.

I remember and never forget that sad day
your suffering ceased and you passed away.
It left me with emptiness and aching heart too
only your smile could make me anew.

In silence and loneliness, I hid away
my grief was in private, not for display.
I went somewhere quiet to go there and cry
and many years later, was still asking 'why?'

MY BEAUTIFUL ROSE

I nursed it and cherished it and fed it with feed
Each day I would run out and just want to see
how my rose looked as it grew in splendour and charm
not wanting anything to do it some harm.

I would smell it and live in its beautiful hue
the colour was stunning, when covered in dew.
My beautiful rose was admired by all
as it stood so erect, proud and tall.

Then one day I looked, with a smile on my face
at my rose, so full of beauty and grace
and noticed a spot on one petal it had
My smile disappeared and I felt quite sad.

The next day another spot came and then more
The leaves, they were withering and looking forlorn.
I started to realise that nothing will last
in this life but to hold that memory fast.

I cut down my rose before it had died
and laid it to rest, as it's beauty did fade
and left me with memories of my lovely flower
Memories last and hold the most power.

The Angel

By the side of the road, one day
an old man begged someone to stay
and talk with him in his loneliness
He longed for peace and was in distress.

Many passed by that road that day
They gave not a glance as they went on their way
busily striving to make ends meet
they cast not a look except at their feet.

Some were rich and had houses and land
Some had plenty within both their hands.
Others were pretending to look away
too busy and rushing to kneel and pray.

The old man was lonely and shedding a tear
as all were too busy to come over here
and talk to him, listening to his complaint
He was so hungry and thought he might faint.

Then along came a child, kicking a ball
saw the old man leaning on the wall
said to him, 'Mister, have one of my sweets',
'I have two left, so it's a treat'.

The old man, he took it and thanked the small boy,
he was so grateful and gave him a toy
The small boy ran home but he looked back then
the old man had vanished and never seen again.

Be careful when looking around as you go
It might be an old man but you never know
dressed up in old clothes, an angel, maybe
Welcome him, talk with him, then you will see.

Smile

Only a smile but the hope that it brings
can last for a life time and make the heart sing.
Sadness around can lower the soul
but a smile has the benefit of making us whole.

Just a smile can bring a shaft of great light
and fill the receiver with endless delight
and warmth and affection and brotherly love
displays the heart's longing and comes like a dove.

A smile is so gentle and sincere in its tone
It welcomes, embraces and feels just like home
It lifts up the spirit and the joy that it gives
when we do receive it helps us to live.

Trust

What do we hope for and in what do we trust?
Is it gold and silver, which end up as dust?

Nothing will last and nothing will stand
only few things which we hold in our hand.

Faith in your God is all that will last.
Trust never ending, like a rock that holds fast.

It cannot be seen and cannot be felt
but it gives us such hope and our hearts have to melt

And soften with gentleness, kindness and giving
gives us great joy and a reason for living

Although we may lose all that we hold dear
the faith that we hold will take away fear.

Fear of the unknown and fear of the death
that comes to us all in one final breath.

Fearful of living and fearful of how
we will survive when the cold wind does blow

and take away everything in which we put trust
Faith in our God is something we must.

Pride

All will crumble, all will fall.
Those that trust in standing tall

Those with pride above their friend
with head held high and a message they send,

that they are important and others see them
and fear them and bow low and take the blame.

All those with pride will come here at last,
stripped of all glory, remembering the past.

With regret and not comfort, they lay in their bed
the tears fall down now. What have they said?

Have they guided others to live like a King?
Or live as a pauper, gaining nothing?

All because their pride would not bend
and bow before others and give them a friend.

COMFORT

Do not be frightened Come and sit by my side
and I'll be your comfort and I'll be your guide.
With my arms around you, I'll hold you so tight
taking away sorrow and easing your fright.
Night turns into day when I sit by your side
being your comfort and being your guide.

THE WRONG PATH

I saw a young man walking through the night
furtively glancing from left to right.
No clear direction, lost in the dark
in the street one minute and then in the park.

What does he do and where does he go?
For what is his life and what does he show?
Parents at home, living life to the full,
enjoying their lot and playing the fool.

It's no little wonder that their son does not know
the direction to go in, as he wanders so slow.
Now he is looking and a window he spies.
The house is so dark and he hears no cries.

The streets are all silent and nothing to do
but climb in and gaze on the things that look new.
He picks up some jewels that lay on the side
it all seems so easy and he takes it with pride.

Where are his parents and what will they do,
as they sit at home and playing the fool.
Laughing and singing and dealing with cards
little do know that their son finds it so hard.

He has had no guidance or someone to follow
wandering the streets and mind feeling hollow.
What does he hear as the burglar alarm
has sounded and now it shatters the calm.

He runs and he runs but there's nowhere to hide
he cannot go home, with tears now he cries
A flashing blue light is all that he sees
as he hides in the park amongst the trees.

He's soon caught fast and held in a jail
he's trembling, now and face has turned pale.
Where is the Dad and the Mum that I knew
when I was so small and worries were few.

"Please won't you help me and give me a break
I did not mean in that house to take
the things that belonged to another, not mine,
while my parents at home, with their friends they did dine.

Dad, please don't hit me and Mum please don't scold
My heart feels so heavy, my spirit so cold.
I took the wrong path and now I must feel
the weight of my guilt when I went to steal."

Little Boy Lost

What do I see in the corner just there,
crouching down low and clothes all a tear.
Trying to avoid all the glances of those,
who study his form from his head to his toes.
Judging him, forming opinion in mind.
Where is the comfort, where is the kind?
Did they not know that his father he feared
the anger he saw, the tears that he shed.
He wanted to be near his Mother's side,
and run to her, feel comfort and with her to hide.
The fear of his father had stopped him from getting so close
to his Mother, as she was the one he loved the most.
Now he's alone and lost in his mind
misunderstood and longing for peace
just one kind look or comfort at least.
Along came an old woman, dirty and poor
she bent down and opened her grimy front door,
suddenly seeing the little boy there
alone in the corner, his mind full of care.
She turned and placed arms around him so tight
his night turned to day and saw the sunlight.
It was not the strong that brought him some peace
but a lonely old woman, with her he found rest.

THE STORM

The storm it raged both day and night
and brought such fear and filled with fright
The sailors wrestled and tried to save
their boat from being smashed in the angry waves.
Look beneath the waves that bring fear
and what do you see and what do you hear?
There's calm and peace and colourful scene
the fish they swim the creatures they move
on the seabed and one thing this proves,
that every storm has a peaceful beneath
if we can find it and we can have faith.

PAIN

It cannot be understood by those
who have no experience of its unnerving pose.
The pain that envelops its arms all around
some and not others and relentlessly pounds

And tears at the soul and spirit as well
making the life seem like something from hell
but there is a light that is seen by its grip
pain is a warning, when from that cup we sip,

whether its mild or whether its strong
it warns us that something is terribly wrong.
It may be that we have from a pathway strayed
or just that our body and mind are afraid.

Or maybe some illness or disease has occurred
leaving our body or mind that is scarred.
So pain can be helpful and kind to us when
we heed its, great warning and see in it a friend.

Agitation

Agitation, stress, worry to what does it lead?
What is the benefit? It plants a small seed.

Which grows and grows into a large tree
where birds cannot lodge and the branches stay free.

No fruit on it grows and the leaves they are brown
some of them fall and are trodden down.

The tree may look tall and so strong as it stands
but the roots are as if they were growing in sand.

The storm winds will blow and the branches will bend
the roots, they will wither and die in the end.

Then all that is left is the stump in the ground
as it rots and decays and cannot be found.

So learn to live without all that is false
and live life to the full and stay on the course.

Business

Rushing here and rushing there
always rushing and filled with care.
Never a moment to stop and look
at the beauty around in the tiniest nook.

Making noise as a demonstration
what others should do, in our frustration.
The body and mind can only take part
of all that we force it to take from the start.

Its training you see from those that do lead
and guide us in life and starts as a seed.
So stop and think twice and embark on a course
that comes out of choice and never from force.

Love

Love is so powerful, love is so kind
affecting the body, soul and the mind.

Enveloping, searching and finding us out
if we are so real or filled with great doubt

About what love is and what does it do
is it for me and is it for you?

Love is for all if they will receive
and learn from its lessons to seek just to give.

Rewards can be great and blessings abound
when we are all giving and love is around.

Care

Care for the elderly, sick and the poor
Care for the one who knocks at your door.

Care for the babe and care for the child
Care for the simple and those that are wild.

So many ways to care for them all
So many ways for the large and the small.

Develop a caring and loving heart
if we only care we play our part.

This world can be rich worth more than choice gold
if we can start caring for the young and the old.

Children

I see a smile, a beautiful smile
as I stop to look and ponder a while.

The smile on the face of a little child
That smile turns sadness to warmth deep inside

as its innocence and friendship can reach to our soul
making us think and making us whole.

The hand is now stretched to take ours in theirs
The touch that we feel, it brings out the tears

As we ponder and realise that we have so much
but a little child leads us by their tender touch.

Time

The clock does not stop but time rushes by
it never stops ticking for you or for I.
Whether we turn to the left or the right,
still time, never ending is not ruled by sight.

We cannot see where it comes and it goes
Where has it gone? Nobody knows.
Use it with wisdom for it never returns
only to haunt fools, for its teaching they spurn.

Choice

"Choose well, choose with wisdom", said the old man one day
as he stumbled along and passed on his way.

Who will listen and who will tell?
Who will heed the wise words so well?

"Life is before us," the young man declared,
as he hurried along, without even a care.
"I want what life offers, with no sacrifice,
no one to tell me, no look to give twice.

Just give me the fun and variety too,
the money, the car." That's all he knew.

The old man walked on with a tear on his cheek.
He'd learned a hard lesson, which left a great mark.

"The young man must learn his own pathway," he thought.
His way he will choose, whatever he's taught.

The Poor Man

The king in his house sat thinking one day,
"What is that bundle of rags by the way?"
"Remove from my gate the untidy disgrace,
my friends will not come to my rich palace."

"Embarrassed, they are by the poor at my gate,"
he said to himself, with his heart full of hate,
for money and riches had blinded his sight
of the real need at his gate of the poor in his plight.

His servants removed the scene at the gate
of the beggar and poor who lay in a state.
With nowhere to go and nowhere to hide
the beggar grew ill and soon he had died.

The rich man lived on in his pride and his wealth,
not assuming for one minute it would soon be his death,
and then the poor beggar would be in comfort of soul,
while the king, with no riches, was a story not told.

FEELINGS

What is this I feel deep down inside of me?
No one can see it and no one knows
it is there. Only I can see
and feel the pain that grows and grows.

I cannot explain it or put it into words
the feelings that I have deep inside.
They entwine around me like a thousand cords
some I reveal and some I hide.

The pain is in my mind and heart.
The secret places I physically feel
an ache inside, which bears a part
of some that I can never reveal.

I cannot escape who I am
or deny the fact that I have failed,
so many people think I'm a sham
on a storm tossed sea within a gale.

When will I be free and when a calm?
When will my boat sail out of the storm?
When will I be home and feel healing balm
out of the cold and into the warm?

FORGIVENESS

I've known forgiveness for all I've done
and all I've said and thought and known.
I've known what it is to feel the pain
of guilt for those I've brought such shame.

God forgives more than we could ever know,
when we do not deserve his love and so
we can only follow his example and then
to love others and forgiveness to send.

To forgive those who have wronged us so much
to give them kind words and a tender touch.
Is worth more than all the riches we own
and then can give life to those who might drown.

H A T E

I saw a young man who was filled with hate
He had no concern for another's fate
He would walk on by from a troubled soul,
His mind was dark and his heart was cold.

He once knew how to love and care
but the world was hard and stripped him bare.
Taking advantage of his tender heart
and thrust him through with their selfish darts.

Now he wandered along the road
out in the cold and carrying a load,
which grew heavier as the years went by
hate turned so bitter, blinding his eye.

The choice he had made was to have his revenge
on a world that he felt had caused him such pain.
If hate is not dealt with and the owner forgives
then others will die when they want to live.

FLYING

The tiny eagle, he sat in the nest
snuggling for warmth in his mother's breast.
The fear was all gone in that peaceful place
fear of the world that he could not face.

He became stronger as he grew
his thoughts of peace and the warmth he knew
was soon to be shattered with new things to come,
that placed him in danger and places of harm

This was necessary to take his place
in a world that was sparing in mercy and grace.
His mother, one day flapped her wings and pushed
him out of the nest and as the wind rushed

by, he fell and fell headlong
it was now that he did not feel so strong.
As he was falling, he wondered 'why?'
His mother expected him to fly,

When she knew he could not, then he found,
just before he hit the ground,
his mother had caught him from underneath
back to the nest he was shaking like a leaf.

When he stopped shaking out once more
from the nest she pushed, with her claw
and he fell again and desperately
flapped his wings so urgently.

All of a sudden, his fall was slowed,
the trembling ceased and then he showed
that he could fly at last and then
he rose to the sky and flew down again.

Soaring higher and higher he flew
There was a gentle breeze, which blew
and lifted him, gliding on its frame
and he now knew he'd never be the same.

This is the moral of this tale,
when you feel down and life's a gale
and tossed upon the stormy seas
you still can fly upon the breeze.

Acceptance

I sit at the feet of the Son of God,
as my tears fall down upon the sod
and my heart is heavy and filled with guilt.
I hang my head with a lowly tilt.

His gentle words, I hardly hear,
as he tries to speak and lift my fear.
His hand is poised upon my chin
and he lifts my head to gaze at him.

Those eyes I see so filled with pain,
the world he loved and bore their stain,
did not accept him and refused
his offer of mercy and his grace.

Now he looked into my eyes
his face so kind and heart so wise.
He did not condemn me on his part
his love alone, that broke my heart.

BEAUTY

Look around and you will see untold beauty in many things.
The beauty of a flower or a blade of grass or a bird that sings.

See the loveliness in the clouds that flow on a gentle breeze,
or the summer sunshine or cold winters freeze.

So much beauty, but there is a beauty that is not often told
not so much the beauty of the young or the grace of the old.

But some have their scars that life has been cruel
they hang down their head and they feel like a fool.

Scars of the mind and body and soul,
feeling a misfit and not one who's whole.

They have a beauty that is all of their own,
not beauty of face or beauty of tone,

but deep down inside where nobody sees
is beauty untold, like the flowers or trees.

STRENGTH

I saw a man of muscular tone
He felt so proud of fitness and one
that was unique in his confident pose
Disciplined mind and body that glows.

Daily he exercised, straining for more
he felt so rich, although he was poor,
no one would challenge his powerful frame
he felt so strong, he'd never be the same.

Other men envied him. Women he loved
all flocked around him. To them he proved
that he was the fittest and strongest of men.
He had what he wanted in women as friends.

Slowly but surely he succumbed to the charms
of envying men and the women he calmed
And he did not know, as with pride that was great
that little by little he did things that he'd hate.

The moral that lies in this tale that is told,
is that strength does not lie in the young or the old,
real strength of the will and the heart we must choose
determined to do good and evil refuse.

The Look

A look can determine many things
a scowl, a frown, a heart that sings.
A look, it can give and enrich someone's life
or steal and take and fill with strife.
A look will expose what the heart is inside
where nobody sees and we want to hide
but look at the eyes and we will all see
something that binds us or sets us so free.

Suffering

We think how much we have suffered and lost
and forget the awful terrible cost
that God has suffered when he came to earth
and many laughed and treated him with mirth.
In life we lose through sin and shame
then wonder where we put the blame
and cry and weep from where we are.
and we feel so hurt and marred.
There's always forgiveness, compassion and care
from one, who loves and our pain he bears
but spare a thought for what he has lost
and suffered and hurt through terrible cost.
Our selfishness, greed, envy and hate
have given God much to bear on his plate,
so next, when you think of the pain you bear
he suffers in silence with no one to care.

Gentleness

I was walking along the street one fine day,
when I saw a young man who was simple in his way.

Others avoided him, they were filled with their cares
going about business, selling their wares.

I saw him stoop to pick up a bird
with broken wing, in the gutter he spied.

He took it home and nursed it to health.
He was poor and had no wealth

but the riches he had, no one could see
they were deep in his heart. He had set the bird free.

Protection

The lion, it crept through the long grass
keeping low, as the little animals pass.
The little ones were with their mother for food
had not a care and life was so good.

The mother sensed that danger was near
and gathered her brood around her in fear.
The lion it seized its chance and it sprang
into action and went for the weakest at hand.

Chasing it, leaping to tear at its throat
the little one cried a pitiful note
but the mother had run as fast as she could
and now in between the lion she stood.

The lion was not to be outdone by the beast,
so attacked the mother and at the very least,
determined to kill her instead of her babe.
but she stood her ground, although was afraid.

She never once altered her stance to protect
her little babe, who cowered in the grass and wept,
as he saw his dear mother torn apart
dying for him, it wrenched at his heart.

The sacrifice that his mother had made
was filling his thoughts as he ran away.
Determined to be brave for others he was,
when he had a family, whatever the cost.

Misunderstanding

What do I think? What do I feel?
What do I say? To hurt or to heal?
It's only when others tell me what I have said,
that I realise the damage done where I have been led.

My motive is pure and wanting the best
but what comes across must take the test
of how it is taken and how it's returned
when it is accepted or when it is spurned.

Remember that all of us are so unique
that we can interpret the words we receive
as offensive or difficult when our heart is maimed
so think very carefully when we want to blame.

See beyond words that are spoken in pain
see the one giving and do not hold blame
Maybe they hurt and are suffering too
how we receive can make them anew.

BRAVERY

Gone is the shame of the mistakes of yesterday.
Or are they really gone? How much do I have to pay?
I only wanted to be brave and serve my fellow man.
What went wrong and do I really know who I am?

Deep inside there is something burning bright,
no one can see it but it illuminates the night.
I know it is there, the honour without shame
but who points the finger, who is there to blame?

One day it will be seen by all with eyes to see
and recognised by those who feel similarly.
But there are those who do not see the end of shame
whose hearts are hard to those without a name.

LITTLE CHILD

Inside all of us there is a little child
in some it is small, in some it is wild.

It may be angry, forsaken and alone
and crave attention and needing a home.

We've grown up now and into adulthood
but still the little child, all alone it stood.

Memories sore and pain that cries aloud
hurting, feeling, the adult head is bowed.

If left, this child will grow into a man
and steal and mar the adult master plan.

It has to die and grief that must be felt
the heart is pained and now it has to melt,

but once the grief and pain is overcome,
the man emerges, as brightly as the sun.

A Man

What is a man? What has he become?
Is he self-centred, with heart as a stone?
Grabbing for gain and climbing the stair
of success and wealth and grasping the air.

Beauty is drained and ugliness shows
when man is a robot that nobody knows.
What man has lost can always be gained
in giving to others and having a name.

The pleasure in giving to make someone great
in this other person, whoever we meet
will make us a man in true sense of the word
the example we set breaks many a cord.

Touch

Let me touch you with heart that is pure
and mind filled with kindness, hands that can cure.
with only a touch but the healing that comes
to heart that is aching and mind that is numb.

The pain that you feel let me bear it now
and take it with hands that are soft on the brow.
But only I know the scarring I feel
in hands that can touch you and longing to heal.

Father

Father, why do you beat me so?
See in my mind, do you not know?

The pain that I feel, the inner turmoil
The guilt and the anger that threatens to soil

My futile and poor life, my lack of self worth.
Why am I living and brought to birth?

I grew from a child and into a man
and then understood how this life plan

of being a father and treat with respect
each tiny child, to love and correct.

Father, dear father look what you've done
oh, how much you've lost in gaining a son.

All because you lost your father too
inflicting your pain was never the cure.

Time

Time never ceases, it never stands still
whether we're well or if we are ill.

If we are young or if we are old
whether we're warm or feeling the cold.

How do we spend time? Once it is gone
it never returns. The path that we're on

turns right or to left or carries on straight
a door on this side, on that side a gate.

Ponder our pathway and which way we turn
for time is a thief, if its wisdom we spurn.

PRISON

Is a prison four walls and bars at the windows?
With a bed, chair and table as we fall so low?

Is it because we fail and break the law?
Do we descend from rich to poor?

A prison can be what around us we see
with punishment and pain, knowing not to be free.

But there's a prison within us that no one can see
no one can know it but who has the key?

We have the power in each of our hands
to lock the door of another's plans.

We turn the key of hate and pain
and lock them into a life so drained

of freedom, love, friendship and calm
we're blinded to truth and only want harm

We all have a choice to throw away the key
nevermore to be found, if only we see

that love and forgiveness can break every chain
within the prisoner, and all of us, healing the pain.

The Book of Life

Some start at the back to see how it ends
others within the pages descend,
While still others will start at the front
and never complete what they want,

All of us have to start where it begins
and walk through its pages, full of our sins.
Emotions and feelings of pleasant or ill
taken without choice of using our will.

We all have to choose where we will start
when we discover what is our part.
Then when we arrive at the close of the book
our head turns around and backward we look

but no one can change the destiny now
when we get to the-end and then we bow
in contrition and regret, if we do not choose
wisely and bravely for a life not confused.

Hospitality

Come in, sit down, if ill or bent
in pain or soiled with good intent.

Let me show you what I can give
to ease your life and make you live.

I will feed you and clothe you too
make you clean and feel brand new.

Washing away all your past
with dirt and filth, then clean at last

You will have all that I can give
of myself to let you live.

Anger

The sea roars and froths and smashes the rocks
determined to kill and steal. In its grip it locks
the mariner, struggling his ship to steer
with sweat on his brow and eyes filled with fear.

His thoughts go afar to long distant shores
Why did he come on this particular course?
His heart now is gripped in panic and afraid
has he forgotten how once he prayed?

He thinks of his wife and children at home
how far he has sailed and how long had he come.
Why did he not think more of her then?
What he would give to be with his friends.

The waves now are-fierce and vast and so high
threaten his boat. The end seems so nigh.
He thinks of the things that he should have done
The ways that he could have played with his son.

The little things now seem so great and so tall
but then, in the past, they were nothing at all.
Now with mast gone and boards that do creak
washed overboard the value he did seek.

He calls to his maker for mercy and grace
and promised if only he saw his wife's face
then all would be different, the values would change
his life would be spared and be rearranged.

The end of this tale was that he did come home
battered and bruised but changed from within.
The mariner had changed but what of the one
who feels the cold anger and blots out the sun?

SURRENDER

To what do we surrender and give up our right?
What shuts out the day and brings in the night?

There are many things that can take away choice
not coming in whispers but with a loud voice.

Sometimes we're willing and sometimes we're not
Sometimes so cold and others so hot.

Forcing, taking, pleasuring the mind
something so cruel, fierce and unkind.

Do not be harsh with those who succumb
The power that's upon them will leave them so numb.

Help them and teach them with wisdom and might
to never surrender or give up their right

to live on this earth as special and unique
achieving their goal, whatever they seek.

HURTING

Why are we hurting? Why do we blame
this one and that one? They're all the same.
Guilty or not, the focus for all
who we are, where we are, the short or the tall.

When we are hurt it is deep within
but someone has blame and others have sin.
If only we knew the healing that comes
from letting it go and let in the sun.

The rays of the sunshine bring healing and calm
to a troubled mind and spirit that wants only harm.
The sunshine we seek is the sunshine of love
coming so gently just like a dove

But if we arrive at the place of true hope
and let love be our aim and help us to cope.
Then we will receive the joy, which we long
and heart that feels light and mouth with a song.

Darkness

Who is that wandering around in the dark?
Can they not see the flowers in the park?
Can they not hear the whispering breeze?
Feel the sunshine and see the trees?

Why can't they see the things that we see,
things that bring pleasure to you and to me?
The darkness they feel is deep within
with eyes they do see but hearts full of sin.

Longing to be free but not knowing how
stumbling around and heads they do bow
In tiredness and weakness and heaviness of soul
asking, why they are here, left out in the cold?

Mum

I loved my Mum, I wish she were here
taking my hand and removing my fear.
She went long ago to far away lands
but I see her face and feel her hands.

She was so gentle and kind that I know
She kept in the background, not wanting to show
others her beauty but only to give
of all that she had, for someone to live.

OLD LADY

There she was, lying alone in her bed
Eyes now were dim, her husband long dead.

Many passed by, living their way
Rushing around but there is one day

that they will be like the old lady in bed,
straining to hear all that is said.

To listen to her when we take the time
whispering her memories of some distant clime

we find we're enriched and filled with an awe
of her knowledge and gentleness. She will open a door,

help us be like her of patience and love,
then one day we will be able to prove

that all of us can enrich so many lives
whatever our state or our age ninety five.

GRANDMA

I went to her room and knocked on the door,
when I was a little boy with eyes on the floor.

Battered and bruised and fearing so much,
I tapped on the door. In my hand I clutched,

a tiny flower with stalk withered and bent.
Some petals were missing but she'd know what I meant.

All I wanted was to give from my heart,
to my dear granny, and play my part.

In her old life so gentle and kind,
frail elderly body but quick supple mind.

The door slowly opened and she peered around,
my heart skipped a beat, I looked at the ground.

But when she had placed her arm around mine,
all fears were gone, all sense of time.

I sat with her listening and loving her voice,
gentle and soft, silencing the noise,

that was in my head, as I sat on her chair.
I loved my old granny, for me she did care.

Parting

We may part for whatever reason
but we cannot silence the memories that came in their season.
Memories of children playing with their Dad
some of good times and others of bad.

The fun and laughter, the games and the tears
the hugs and the kisses that silence the fears.
Memories of lost ones held dear to our heart,
the days we were weeping and playing our part.

Naughty things that our children did
reminding us when we were a kid.
Struggles and pain to raise up our own,
reaping in their lives, just what we've sown.

So many holidays and picnics too
games on the beach, then just me and you.
Our children are now gone. Don't throw it away
memories of good times, of work and of play.

BITTERNESS

A tiny seed drops into the ground.
Nourish it, water it and see what is found.
It is no bother, leave it alone.
It will not harm, it is like a stone,

With no life or movement it lies as dead
but then a tiny root like a thread
winds its way down through the soil.
It cannot be seen and we can be foiled

in our efforts to ignore its tiny ways
with now more roots on sun filled days.
Disguised, it now bursts through the sod
stretching upwards towards its god;

which is domination and achieves its aim
when we believe it is a game.
We do not take it seriously now
until before it we humbly bow.

As it takes over all that is good,
all that is healthy, our daily food.
We crave its attention and wonder why,
our hearts are dark and our minds are tired.

When it has taken our home away
it invites its friends to come and stay.
in visits jealousy, envy and pride
not to be noticed they hide inside,

And enjoy the freedom of living alone
communicating well. The owner has gone.
He is outside his own hearts desire
gone is the warmth and gone is the fire.

Stubbornness now knocks at the hearts door
loving the pride, no regard for the poor.
Invited inside he sits down with ease,
loving no one, himself he will please.

Given their reign they will tear us apart
Then at the end, will thrust in their dart,
so do not go down the road that they share
they'll toss you aside without a care.

Lying

It sounds like the truth but don't be deceived
subtle it is and cannot be believed.
Better to be honest and consequence take
than lying and cheating, really a fake.

The cost involved in telling the whole
will clear your mind and heart and soul
and you will live in freedom, though
the truth may hurt as everyone knows.

Stealing

Do not take what is not your own
You may be taking some other throne,
many a thing that is not yours by right
can damage and hurt and bring on the night.

Many things precious to one just may seem
trivial to another and look so mean
but another man's poverty is another's wealth
and one act of stealing can ruin the health.

So be careful before you are tempted to steal
what belongs to another. You have power to heal
and give to another and not to take
if not only for them but for your sake.

ON SOLID GROUND

One day an old man stood alone on the rocks
He had taken the beating and taken the knocks
Laughed at and harassed because not the same
as others around him, but he's not to blame.

His face was disfigured, and hair had not grown
when he was a baby, ever since he was known.
He heard the loud roaring of waves as they crashed
at his feet exploding on the rocks, they smashed.

But try as they could, they could not move those
rocks that were solid on the beach as they froze.
This reminded the old man, persecuted sore
no man could move him, if like the rocks on the shore.

FAMILY

No matter what happens or where we go wrong,
family will always return to where they belong,
Whatever, as parents we taught them to be,
wherever they go in life they always see.

The standards they're taught when young and as they grow,
deep in their minds the thoughts parents have sown.
How they are disciplined when they are young,
will keep them upon the path and then among,

all the right people whose lives can enhance,
their life, giving their children a new chance.
As generations come and generations go,
we should be careful whatever we sow.

Seeds cannot grow if the soil is no good,
and lives can be lost for want of good food.
Therefore it shows that we teach what we know,
and pass on to others, what they can then sow.

Broken Promises

We all have dreams and broken promises
and all have things that we have said
and not done. We place them in a large bin
at the bottom, hidden among our other sin.

Some admit their guilt and the bin is bare
while others pretend they are not there.
The bin is large, unclean, and quite full
with things that make us look a fool.

There's shame, embarrassment, guilt and pain
empty hopes and clothes all stained.
There's only one way to empty them out
and that is known without a doubt,

to be honest and admit when you are wrong
Put the past behind you and journey along.
Be determined to keep your word
with promises made that you can afford.

A Hug

What does it cost to hug someone?
When they are feeling all alone
and cannot make it through each day,
not knowing if to go or stay.
Blind and fearful clutch at straws
they have tried so many doors
but many slam shut in their face
and they walk away in disgrace.
Sometimes angry, sometimes sad,
sometimes wondering at what they had.
Now they ache for life's embrace
but no one comes to this small space.
Please, oh, please will someone give
just a hug that I might live.

SUNSHINE

The sun shines through the windowpanes
and lights up my pictures held fast in their frames.
One of my treasures, grand-daughter so dear,
smiling and laughing with face full of cheer.

Other prints framed with greatest of care
one over here, another over there.
There is my wife with eyes full of grace
the sunlight shines in and lights up her face.

I sit and I gaze at this beautiful sight
and wonder how life brings us to a sad plight
of memories sore and pain deep inside.
Secrets we can tell and others we hide.

PASSING BY

What is that bundle of rags that I see
just over there by yonder tree?
I catch someone's arm as they hurry by
but they hurry on, and I wonder why.
Another, I speak to was all in a rush
'Sorry' they say, as they try to hush
my inquisitive nature, as puzzled
I stand and slowly let go of their hand.
I go to the bundle and just as I thought
a man lay there with bottle of port
in his hand and clothes all torn
looking sad and so forlorn.
He had come from fine house and wife
now had met with many a strife.
To the gutter sunk as low as he was
memories painful and counting the cost.
I looked with pity at this poor man

dirty and drained and empty hands.
No one wanted him and no one cared
if he lived or died. His life was spared
and I watched as I sat there by his side,
as they all passed by on the other side.

SPEED

The wheels spin and dust flies in the air
faster, faster, without a care.
The heart beats faster, the wind rushes by
I'm moving so fast, I'm sure I could fly.
Foot hard to the floor with adrenaline rush,
palms now sweating and face is a flush.
Thoughts are racing of the pace of life
job secure, home and a wife.
Money in the bank and children at play,
holidays later, so easy to pay.
Dream on, young man with excitement around.
The speed is tremendous, the car leaves the ground.
Now the mood changes and terror will strike
'I was only having fun, like I did on my bike'
but now things are different power is there
under the bonnet, out in the air.
'Please don't let me die, I just want to live
my life and then others receive when I give.'
Over and over, the car spun around,
hitting the air and then on the ground.
Finally coming to rest in a field
dented and battered and smashed windshield.
'Am I alive?' 'Yes, bleeding, I fear'
taken to hospital, there for a year.
When he went home, with crutches and limp,
safe to his family and wife, made him think
of what were priorities, relationships, and friends,
so much more valuable than money and things.

My Dear Son

Wherever you go, whatever you do,
I may not like it but it is you
that is important to me and so
what means so much to me, wherever you go,
is that you are my son and you know
that you will always be welcome at my side.
Do not be afraid and run away and hide
or hang your head and stand to one side
in shame and disgrace, for there will always be
a home to share for you and me.
I am proud to call you my son
and I know that you are the one
who will blossom one day into all that you can be
and I shall be so proud that others will see
your achievements and hopes come into view.
I know you have so much within you
so do not be ashamed but hold your head up high,
and walk forward and do not be shy.
Then one day you will know you are the one
that I have always loved, for you are my son.

Beautiful Daughter

You were so tiny and on others depend
when you were born. God chose to send
you to our home. The pleasure that we knew
in just loving and caring for you,
will always be there in our minds.

Then as you grew, you were so kind
and naughty too, just as a child
the discipline we gave was mild,
for you were sensitive and caring
encouragement you were not sparing.

Soon into a young woman you grew
and fell in love with someone new,
and then you chose your wedding dress.
The great day came, with share of stress,
and you prepared to be the bride,

but only when you came outside
your room and down the stairs did glide,
you would have noticed a tear in my eye.
You were so radiant and beautiful, yet
as long as I live, I will never forget.

Memories

As I think back long ago
to times when we were wed and so
the years went by and troubles too
came and went but knowing you
was worth it all if only this
could last with memories deep inside
of many things that pleasure brought
and joy so deep it cannot be bought.
What has happened to our love
we had together when we proved
to many standing round who saw
that we had something rich, not poor
in our relationship, but then
it was snatched away in pain.
No one can remove the thoughts
that within my mind, not sought,
they're always there day and night,
treasures that I hold so tight.
We walked along the sand and dined
together many times, shared wine,
but the best times were spent with you
wherever we went and whatever to do.

Destiny

Where have we come from? To where do we go?
Who is our master? Who is our foe?
For what is our life worth if no goal is found?
No vision, no future, we look to the ground.

Lift up your eyes and see what is beyond,
What fills our gaze and for what do we long?
There is something far greater and nobler by far
to sacrifice life and limb for others without war.

Our destiny lies in our hands if we yield
to giving and sharing and many we heal,
and then, when at last we lay down our tired life
we shall be satisfied to go without strife.

God's Plan

God has a plan for each of our lives.
We try to live properly, struggle and strive,
earnestly seeking to be so good
in our own efforts if we could.
But try as we may it seems doomed from the start.
We all make mistakes, damage other hearts.
The level of morals is our own that we set
and not someone else's standard, and yet
we do not see truth when in front of our eyes,
that God's standard is best, in him is no lies.
He wants the best for each of our lives,
we have no need to struggle in anguish and strive
but just let him live through us, working his plan
and then at the last we become a new man.

Empty

We sometimes seem empty, with nothing to give,
All power is drained from us, we don't seem to live.

We have given so much and sacrifice too,
now we seem empty, battered and bruised.

Some have abused us and others ignored,
our offer of kindness but we are assured,

that somewhere so deep down in our heart,
is a hidden treasure to play another part.

Just when we think there is nothing at all,
gold dust is hidden to help us stand tall.

The Churchyard

All was silent and all was calm
there in the churchyard as the choir sings a psalm
in the church but just outside
in the corner, no room for pride,
a woman kneels by the grave that she tends,
seeking an answer and seeking a friend.
This was her son and the only one too
one that she loved more than we knew,
taken in prime of life so suddenly
an accident happened as he struck a tree,
He died in the hospital as he lay on the bed,
and to his dear mother he whispered and said
'I love you Mum, I don't want to die,'
then closed his eyes, with Mum by his side.
Now she's alone and tears falling down,
Kneels in the dirt, her face wears a frown,
when suddenly felt a hand on her arm
gently touching her and making her calm.
A voice said to her, 'I understand your pain,
and the hurt that you suffer, I went through the same.'
She looked up with gratitude at the stranger she heard,
but no one was there, just the singing of the birds.

Goodbye

In the hospital bed lay a tired old man,
his heart, it was failing, his life had it's span.

He had been told that his time was so short,
no time to travel, just time for thought.

'Where is my dear wife?' he said as he lay,
longing for her touch and hearing her say,

'thank you for life and the time we were wed,
now your suffering alone in your bed.'

That night the nurse pulled the curtain around.
The wife stayed all night, took her feet off the ground

and cuddled her dear husband as he breathed his last,
saying goodbye, with thanks for the past.

This true story was told with tears in the eyes
of the person who told it, touched deep inside.

Disappointment

Excited, longing full of such hope
life is so good, able to cope,
the plans that were made for just a few things
to see my grand-daughter play on the swings.
Something so small, insignificant now,
means so much to me. In my mind I vow,
I'll never for granted take little things I enjoy,
especially grandchildren, little girl or boy.
Children can bring a wealth of such joy
whether they laugh or play with their toys.
Now it is raining and I cannot meet
my little grandchild. I glance at my feet,
with eyes on the ground and sadness inside,
I hope that the next time comes in like a tide.

Patience

No matter what comes, no matter how hard
life is or if I am dealt a card
that is not too pleasant or comes as a shock
or if I am dealt a blow and take a hard knock
or if some are cruel and treat me unkind
and hurt me inside my heart and my mind.

I have to forgive and have patience with those
who are learning the same lessons and whose
mind is the same and they have their hurts,
so very unsure of life, not sure where to start.
Have patience with all, for we all have our trials,
go with them further, the extra mile.

Strike

Life is too short to spend it lashing out
aggressively, for the pain we have now
we blame others and seek to hurt
whether by deed or by word.

Misunderstanding is so often the key
that causes so much pain to you and to me,
and often the cause of many a fight
to sleep in the day and go through the night.

When we want to strike and lash out at some
and take little thought of wrong things we have done,
the ones who suffer are not those that we hit
but ultimately our health, when our anger is lit.

Kindness

Be gentle be kind, guard your mind
from thoughts of anger and being unkind.
Treat others how we would like them to do
to us, by kindness of many or few.

A kind word or touch can cause to heal
so many who live but cannot feel
but compassion, gentleness, kindness and love,
can break every barrier and cold hearts can move.

Bad Apples

It only takes one in the basket of fruit
to corrupt the rest, as it takes root
and unseen settles amongst the good
spreading its poison wherever it could.
The apples were fresh upon the tree
Growing and taking life so free.
Then they were picked when ready
and ripe placed in a basket, shiny and bright
but one bruise was unseen, as among the rest
under the surface it did its worst.
The apples were stored, 'til after the fall
they would be eaten and enjoyed by all
but as they were taken one by one
the one that was rotten, its deed was done.
Many were scattered upon the dung heap
only a few did the farmer keep
the poison had spread to the good from the bad
all because one was unnoticed and dead.
If we allow the small things in our lives
that may appear pleasant and something to give
but look underneath and see what is there
they will rob you and leave you with cupboard so bare.

Nourish and cherish the things that are good
wholesome and pleasant, enriching for food,
feeding your body and soul will bring peace
and joy to your spirit, with heart full of grace.

The Valley

Whether we're young or whether we're old
we all have to walk that way of shivering cold,
the way of the valley at some time in our life,
the way of true darkness, trouble and strife.
If it is seen as a positive step,
to walk through the valley, though losing our grip,
we hang on to faith in a future more bright
than the darkness we feel as black as the night.
Though paths may be separate, as we stumble along,
we still have our hope that will end in a song,
then as we emerge into sunlight at last
we shiver at the thought of deaths icy blast.
The paths that before were separate and alone
have now merged together and become as one,
we find we are walking with others of like mind
a bond of love is joining, hand in hand we find.
In weakness we entered the valley of doubt
the pain of the darkness caused us to shout,
but now as we gain the solid ground,
we stand tall and firm and strength has been found.
So do not despair when all seems so black
we all walk together and never look back.

DADDY MY FRIEND

I remember when I was only five,
thrilled with my Daddy and being alive,
we would do painting and making things
and he settled me at night as he started to sing.

There on the beach as he held my hand
paddles in the sea and walks on the sand,
he held me so close and we laughed and we played,
made me so calm and so unafraid.

One day I sat playing at home with my toys,
my mother advised me to make some less noise,
for Daddy was ill and lay in his bed,
I went in to see him and to me he said,

'Darling, my darling, my sweet little girl,
Don't be afraid, my little pearl,
I do feel so ill but I'll always be there,
to hold you with comfort and my love to share.'

My Daddy grew worse as each day went by,
I hurt deep inside as on his bed he did lie,
then one night outside, a flashing blue light
lit up the darkness, a frightening sight.

They carried my Daddy on a portable bed,
and stopped as they passed me and to me he said,
'Goodbye, my little one, my angel, my friend,'
and then he kissed me as to me he did bend.

That was the last time I saw my dear Dad,
but one thing I'm sure and of this I am glad,
that I had five years of such fun with my friend,
the love I've been given will never end.

Now through my life as I think on those years,
think of the fun and the laughter and tears,
I miss him so much, miss his loving embrace,
his smile and his laughter, always with grace.

No one will know the pain that's so deep
when my lovely Daddy went on his long sleep,
but one day meet him and then I will send
a message that thanks him for being my friend.

My Lovely Mum

You were always there and welcomed me home
asked me with interest how my day had gone,
you never failed to show me you cared,
knelt by your bed and my safety in prayer.
You worked so hard to love me and gave
all you could to me, though you had to save
hard to economise for two daughters and son,
were so expensive, more than just one.
You lost your husband and our father too,
you did not deserve the pain that you knew,
always so hospitable, so loving and kind
to all who came to your home did not mind.
Thank you my Mum for caring so much,
giving and loving with your tender touch.

The Past

Understand your past and you will find
you can leave it all behind,
with courage and bravery, grace and strength
face the future at length.

The lessons learned will all be true
to benefit me and encourage you.
Valuable lessons, pain severe
when understood the pathway is clear.

We never know the reasons why
but we will understand by and by
and be able to bury past doubts and fears
trouble and tempest, the pain and the tears.

The Secret Mind

Hidden inside the secret mind,
discover it and you will find
a wealth of happiness and joy
along with rubbish you employ.

Reveal the secret mind to one
whose life is bleak, has shut out the sun,
you bring to them new hope and faith
from your experience, love and grace.

Don't hide away and hold it tight
for some it can light up the night,
to share and give from what you have
within your mind, you'll be glad you gave.

Grandad

I miss you grandad, as I stand by your grave,
so much you had and so much you gave,
enriching my life with your kindness and love,
what I have gained from you, now I can prove.

My tears falling down, dear grandad forgive
me for the times when I did not want to live
like you did for all that you wanted to lift
from me, in worry. You were a wonderful gift.

Grandad, remember the times that we had,
times of such laughter, when I was so glad.
Why were you taken, when I loved you most?
It must be that God picked his favourite rose.

Vulnerability

What is this strength on which you rely?
The mask that is yours hides vulnerability.
You stand like a soldier erect and tall,
never admitting that you could fall.

Upon yourself is intolerable strain
if you don't admit the inner pain,
that's deep down inside your frail lonely self,
why not share feelings, don't be left on the shelf.

It's a lonely life when we hide behind masks,
isolated and crying, strong to do tasks
but inside so weak and longing to share
but afraid to do so and lay ourselves bare.

False security lies in our mask,
tear it away, be vulnerable at last,
then when you do so you find with surprise,
you're not alone, with others likewise.

The Boat

The boat is on the stormy sea,
lashed by winds so pitifully,
threatened to sink our craft so frail,
then we shall drown, our lives will fail.

Lift up your eyes and give a thought
to others who in their boat are caught,
in life's cruel sea and tossed about,
filled with pain and fear and doubt.

Your boat is bigger than you think
when you realise we all shall sink,
unless we pull somehow together
and help each other, whatever the weather.

Friend

When through the storms and troubles of life,
filled with pain and filled with strife,
we think we're alone with no one at hand,
no one to bring us safely to land.

There is a friend who stands by our side,
whatever the storm or pain that we hide,
never alone if he is the one,
that holds our hand and brings out the sun.

He never promised a life full of ease,
a life filled with sunshine, relaxed by the sea,
but one thing he promised is never to go
from our side if we trust him to do so.

All that we go through and all that of pain,
he's been there before us and knows of our strain,
so do not be frightened and rush all alone
and leave him behind and blot out the sun.

Loneliness

Why do you lock me away in this room?
Why do you hurt me and leave me alone?
I know I have failed and hurt other lives,
and know that I have been wrong and hurt my own wife.
What is the punishment now I must bear?
Alone in this prison with no one to share.
Friends all desert me and leave me alone,
family don't understand, once we've gone wrong
but there is one who still cares, who created the sun
that shines on our lives and no one he'll shun.
If we only ask him to give us his grace
he comes with forgiveness and love in his face,
he never will leave us and stays with us still
when others have left us to die in our filth.

REMINDERS

Many remind us of past weaknesses
past failures and damage and where we caused stress,
reminded of the steps we took to get here
the way we fell down and huddled in fear.

We have to climb out and walk without dread
from depths so low that we seemed as dead,
nevertheless we can climb if we will
out of the valley and up the first hill.

We all make the journey, so be patient and kind
to those that have hard times and not easy to climb.
Life is not easy to any of those
who left the known pathway and another they chose.

One day we'll all get there, so do not be afraid,
as we are all climbing and some have just stayed
on the right course through life, and never fail
to be honest and true through every gale.

How is it possible to never go wrong?
Never to falter and be without song?
Be true to yourself and you will find
love deep in your heart and peace of mind.

One Word

Only one word, that's all it takes
to give some encouragement, some peace to make,
to spread some tiny glimpse of hope beyond this
to give to another the tiniest kiss.

One word can go far if given in love
given from the heart with nothing to prove,
no selfish motive and nothing to hide
just wanting to give and love without pride.

Looking around we see many who need
just that one word of love without deed.
When some are so discouraged, the tiniest thought
can bring them such peace. for so long they had sought.

Dream

Where is reality? What is a dream?
Dreams are unpleasant, or so it seems,

Waking up in the morning at last
I feel the cold and icy blast.

The dream was another world of flying and fun,
reality is stark and blots out the sun.
In my dream I see faraway lands,
oceans and rivers, a walk on the sand.

I smile in my dreams and laugh and fly
but when I wake up I turn and cry.

Maybe one day this will all end
and there from my dream, I take a friend

into reality, dark as it seems
and turn my reality into my dreams.

Waking

Open your eyes. What do you see,
there upon waking for you and me?
We are all different and see things our own
some are laughing and some wear a frown.

We look to the future and some look with dread
some turn over and sleep instead.
We all have to face our particular day
walking through it in our own special way.

Choices

The right to choose, wrong or right
no man can take from us, though they may fight
to remove our will in power and strength
it cannot stand and will at length
fall into ashes at their feet,
for they have a right, their will to meet,
but give respect to others choice
and let them speak and use their voice
no matter what they have said or done
they all have freedom, everyone.

Outcome

The choices we make and the things that we do
the outcome of this may be something new,
for we have to live with each other, I know
and cannot live for self only to show.
All we do or say someone else will affect
and may alter our lives when with them we connect,
because all of us here in the human race
may look different and have different face
but think what we are and take care what we do,
considering others as well as you.

Hardness

Your heart is so cold and hard, full of hate.
Your mind is filled with confusion of late.
You rush this way and stumble along,
the joy you once knew has long gone.
You hit at the weak and lose many friends
the voice that you speak and the letters you send,
have kept you so bitter, will it ever end?
Let it all go and give your body a break,
for in all this strife inside it you make,
your bones are creaking and your heart it does melt.
When was the last time your kindness felt?
Let others love you, don't push them away.
They want to help you, come what may.
The bitterness came when you were hurt in defeat
but somewhere inside you there's a heart that still beats.
So reach deep down and allow it to rise;
looking to others and taking your eyes
off yourself. Then what do you see?
A cold heart now melted and filled with such peace.

GRIEF

Allow yourself time to cry and to grieve
whatever the pain and hurt that you leave
and whatever the reason you need to let out
the pain now in tears, or voice with a shout.

Be honest and true to yourself and then you
will know true freedom from the feeling of gloom
and hurt that's inside. It will all drift away
in time, if you walk through it into the day.

'Tis a pathway we all tread at some time in life,
we lose something precious like husband or wife.
The lonely pathway that you will now tread
can open your heart again and bring life from the dead.

LITTLE BROTHER

My little brother, so helpless and frail,
crying and lonely, face very pale.

Heart that was damaged, life hung by a thread.
Would he now live, or would he be dead?

This was the question I asked as I went
off to my school, that day that was spent

in faraway thought, my mind not on work
and when it was time, I rushed home on my bike.

As soon as I entered the door of my home,
my father's face looked so very glum,

he did not say before I knew what
had happened and knew that this was our lot.

My little brother died but smiled as he lay
there on his bed, so ill on that day.

The pain deep inside I feel as I write
how I got through that day and that night,
I do not know but one thing's for sure,
I'll see him again in a land that's so pure.

My Darling Mum

I had just left school and started to work
my Mum was in hospital and so I did walk
to go in and see her and give her a note.
I entered the ward with a lump in my throat,
and walked to her bedside, she'd had her op'
now so still and quiet, how did she cope
with all the tubes and oxygen mask?
I was so shocked as she lay on her bed
and wondered if she was living or dead.
She did get well in the months that went by,
my darling mother to love I did try,
but failed many times to show how I felt
towards her. My heart it does melt
whenever I think of her, now in the past,
now she is resting asleep at the last.
Through the next years she grew much worse,
suffering in silence as disease took its course,
sometimes I'd lay with my ear to my floor
above her room and listen or stand at the door.
I knew she was suffering and there I would lay
and hear her cry out in agony and pain,
alone in her room below mine and my heart
was broken in pieces as pain played its part.
Many more times into hospital she went,
'til one final time the ambulance was sent.
Now she was so weak and frail on that day
so very thin and wasted away,
then, when I saw her for the very last time,
so many round her bed, I could not find
a moment to tell her just what I felt,
how much I had loved her but what life has dealt
will stay with me always and not go away,
a measure of comfort I get when I pray,

The Mist of Yesterday

Then it was Christmas time, Dad came in the room
and pulled back the curtains and I knew it was time.
Mum passed away in that hospital bed
and inside my heart, I felt just as dead.
My darling Mum was cold and so still,
now free from her pain and being so ill.
I went into loneliness and cried by myself,
no one was with me, no one to help,
and there, as I stood by her grave side so still,
hearing the birds with their songs that were so shrill,
I asked 'why' oh 'why' did she have to go
and leave me so lonely, I did not know.
When she was alive, I loved her so dear
but I was so weak, I could not get near.
Even now as tears roll down my face,
I long for peace and God's good grace,
but all that I feel, as he takes my hand
is his own love, as he says to me, 'I understand'.

My Friend

Every child has a friend we may not know
This friend stays with them wherever they go.

We cannot see them and feel them like those
who understand in their mind when they feel lost.

When I was young and alone in my bed,
I'd pull up the covers right over my head

and draw imaginary pictures on my sheet,
to show my friend whenever we meet.

My friend and I knew just what I had drawn,
this was our secret, since I had been born.

Many times I withdrew to my mind
to visit my friend as he was so kind.

Now I am grown and do not need my friend,
so he has withdrawn and I, he did send

to walk on through life and face it alone
with only the memories of such a one,

who was always available whenever I need,
he enriched my life and planted a seed,

that would always be with me wherever I go,
this seed, so tiny would grow and grow.

When I am older and my life nears the end,
I know I will still have my available friend.

Children

Children around me, that's all I ask,
when I am sleeping or doing a task,
if I am sad or happy or glad
or if I am lonely and feeling quite bad.

What does it cost for these little ones here?
Those that can lift the heart and take away fear.
Those that are innocent and smile when they wish,
and no matter who you are they give you a kiss.

They do not judge or condemn without doubt
and hold onto your hand if indoors or out.
Please, never remove from me children so dear,
or I will be half the man sinking in fear.

Magic

What is magic with its cleverness and skill?
Make things disappear at will.
Lift the rabbit out of the hat,
set the bird free, hide the cat.

Those that rise and sawn in half,
conjuring tricks, cards and laugh.
There is a magic that many miss,
a gentle smile or tiniest kiss.

A butterfly settles on a colourful flower,
the gentle bird sings, they have no power.
Only the power to touch the soul,
so listen to this magic, not often told.

Thunder and Lightening

The thunder roars with the lightning strike,
toppling a tree and causing such fright.
Running for shelter from wind and rain
and fearful noise and inner pain.

Flashing here and flashing there,
Where will it strike? Please tell me where?
No one will know the end result
of lightening fierce wrath and thunderbolt.

All we feel is the fear within
when caught in its terror and noisy din
but we can watch through the windowpane
of our life's house and remain the same,

secure in the knowledge that whatever is done,
the fate that returns to blot out the sun,
is out of our hands and another's will,
we awake to find we are living still.

My History

My history is so valuable to me,
but its value you cannot see.

Perhaps that is why you do not think,
when you gather my things with a blink.

What to you seems so trivial and slight,
in a moment is lost in the night.

But please take great care
for the tiniest share,

for the letter so torn and so marred,
has a stamp on my mind, which is scarred

with memories, so fragile and frail,
in things all musty and stale.

Some you have lost and some you have burned,
why is it that my life you have spurned?

Is it punishment for things I have done?
So much hurt and pain under the sun.

When will it end? When will you forgive?
When we're destroyed or choosing to live?

The Past

The past is gone and cannot return.
Cannot be relived and some must be burned.
Memories good and memories bad,
sometimes happy and sometimes sad.
Many regrets and many a success,
love and hate and tidy the mess.
For all we do and think and say
and rewind the clock and kneel and pray,
and hurt and pain and feel the blight
that stands and haunts our long dark night,
nothing will change the years gone by,
we live for the future with a sigh.
There are some things that we can change,
years we have left we can rearrange.

Misunderstanding

There is isolation in being misunderstood,
with frustration and loneliness, we try to be good
but even when trying, we fail and fall
and stumble, when we were standing so tall.

In the place of failure, we are blamed for some things
we have not committed, the thought of it stings
but nevertheless it will all come out right,
by not fighting back with strength and with might.

The human heart is baying for blood
and some recompense to wallow in mud
and grind into dust the one who has failed,
wishing that they afar away sailed.

Although they would vanish and go far away,
the one who is hurt and still has to stay
is facing a future with heart dark and cold,
unless they forgive and break the world's mould.

Sentimental Things

I saw a man cry as he looked
through an old box that he took
from a dusty corner in the loft.
Some thought he was so soft
and others thought he was weak
without the ability to speak
with interest and ambition,
but with simple contrition.

As he fumbled through the crumpled pages
and little things that were mouldy through ages,
he was all alone, as he wanted to be
in this secret moment of memory.
Others did not understand
the things that were precious and in his hand
but to him, as he held them near to his heart,
and tears fell down, he never would part
with these letters of old
and secret things that nearly were sold.

Impatience

What is that noise I hear?
Buzzing in my ear?
The elderly man was calling for help
as he had fallen with a yelp
and now lay crumpled in a heap.
He only wanted his dignity to keep
but now, as he lay by the sink,
his arm was cut and he did stink.
'Why do they not come?' he wondered in vain,
the workers drank tea, thought he was a pain,
so never went quickly to help him up,
'til they had drained the very cup.
The old man lay and started to cry.
He could not understand the reason why,
but he was not the one whose patience was thin,
or the one who had committed a sin.

Selfishness

Don't give up your seat for the pregnant mum,
or open the door for the elderly one,
or see them safely across the street
when they're blind or lame, without use of their feet.

Do not say 'thank you' for the slightest thing
or 'please' as you ask with a grin
Do not smile as you wish them 'good day',
or bid them 'God speed' as they pass on their way.

Never give up what is rightfully yours,
or lift someone up as they're down on 'all fours'.
Don't pick up their shopping as it rolls out of their bag,
or let someone go first as their legs start to sag.

Look after 'number one', then if anything's left
you can give to the lame and the blind and the deaf,
but strangely enough your happiness goes
and you feel so wretched from your head to your toes.

Beggar

The old man sat begging by the side of the road,
the woman shuffled past with a heavy load,
even a young man cast out of his home,
from parents and warmth, to this place had come.
Rags on their backs and no shoes on their feet,
'please' they are asking to all that they meet.
Many walk by with scorn and disgust,
'why do they grovel and bow in the dust?'
'when government helps with funding and cash,
why do they beg and embarrass us like this?'
'why don't the police clear the streets and make safe
from all these beggars, strays and waifs?'
All these that were begging had a common bond,

the old and the young or someone's son.
They all stayed together and shared what they had
the little food and warmth they were glad.
Those that walked by with superior stance,
had not the same and cast not a glance.

The Tiny Flame

There was an old cottage near the waters edge,
where an old man lived and it was his pledge
to light a candle every night
in the window; just a little light.
He remembered his father long ago,
who gave his life, when a rope did throw
to someone drowning and sinking fast
and eventually his father did cast
himself into the swirling sea
when his wife expected him home for tea.
The drowning man was saved and free
but the father lost his life. Now he
would burn this light for many eyes
to see just where the land lies.
Our light may be unnoticed and wee
but to some who are drowning, it can set them free.

The Gift

Birthdays come and Christmas too,
with many gifts for me and you.
Gifts that bring laughter and joy
for every little girl and boy.

Adults smile and thanks all round,
when paper's off and present's found,
things that last for many a year,
clothes to wear, the latest gear.

There is one gift for rich or poor
that comes to everybody's door,
of life itself and often health
worth more than all our richest wealth.

Waste

Life can be filled with laughter and fun,
days are spent laying in the sun.
Drinking too much and driving so fast,
giving no thought for the time that is past.

One day we look in the mirror and see,
one grey hair, then two and three,
aches in our joints and a twinge or two,
spots and pimples and feeling blue.

Where is our youth with such fun and laughter?
Gone are our sons and then our daughter,
married with children of their own,
now it is quiet and we're alone.

Now is the time when we look back
with some regrets and things we lacked
but all is not wasted in life before,
we've brought up our children, when we were poor.

The flush of our youth was lessons learned,
and bringing up children took all we earned
but when we think back with grateful heart,
nothing we'd change. We played our part
different to others with differing taste
but we did our best, which was not a waste.

Looking

The old woman took hold of her dustpan and brush,
she was looking for something beneath all the dust.
Down on her knees she brushed this way and that,
bumping her furniture, knocking the cat,
scraping her knees, scratching her hands,
she seemed so anxious with what she had planned.

Looking and looking and searching around,
up on the shelf and then on the ground.
She suddenly heard a knock on the door
and she had been looking for an hour or more
but she shuffled along to see who it was,
her neighbour was there and asked what she lost.

She scratched her old head in puzzled look now,
blinking her eyes and wiping her brow,
she replied to the neighbour, 'I think I do not
know why I am looking for I had forgot.'

Realisation

We notice the sun and look at the moon,
the stars, they shine as if playing a tune;

everything works in harmony, when
we stop to notice it now and then.

We see the flowers, trees so grand
as little creatures run on the ground we stand.

Every movement, every thought
all that from our childhood taught.

Choices to make for good or bad,
grateful for all the things we had.

Rushing here and rushing there,
the pattern painted in each life of care,

all slots together in a daily plan,
a purpose designed for every man.

Slow the carriage and the heart will rest
and discover each plan for the very best.

Minds in turmoil become dizzy and
we only realise when we stop and stand.

Goal

Look to the horizon, there's always a goal,
a place where love is, out of the cold.
Somewhere that hope dwells and mercy for all
and somewhere that longs for each to answer the call.
Do not be discouraged, although all seems lost
and life is so painful and you are counting the cost,
each step is weary, as eyes glance to the feet,
we can see the goal in whatever we meet.
Just lift up your eyes and look straight ahead,

see sun bursting through dark clouds and colour instead
of black and white and grey in your view,
and hopelessness, futility and failure too.
Inner eyes are so powerful they pierce through the cold
and ice of tomorrow, from fear they make bold.
It just takes an action and when the first step
is taken, the darkness will start losing its grip,
the sunshine will warm you and give you new hope
and help you face life's challenge, give grace to cope
with whatever lies before you as no one knows
what is planned for tomorrow but as confidence grows,
the face wears a smile again, the jigsaws in place,
each piece will come together, moulded by grace.

Wedding Day

Look into the eyes and see what is there,
words are now silent; all is laid bare,
as honesty and truth are expressed in the gaze,
with love and compassion, the fire is ablaze.

Think very carefully on what is now said
as many more years are lying ahead;
years of success, sometimes failure too
but with hearts of forgiveness, all is kept new.

Always be open, talk much with each other
as you are now closer than a sister and brother,
hand joins in hand with a touch of healing and love,
as this is the way of our Father above.

When troubles come and threaten your boat,
and thunder and lightning cannot keep it afloat,
cling to each other with all that you have,
though your boat sinks, each other will save.

Love is much higher than silver or gold,
and will increase as the story unfolds,
may many long years be your portion too
as you walk in the light, blessing many, not few.

Friends

Friends may come and friends may go
but there is one friend that I know,
the one who sticks by us whatever goes wrong,
whatever is dark to silence the song.

Wealth unimportant, when that friend's around,
our ability to give does not give ground
to their friendship because it relies on one thing
and that is inside them, the ability to sing.

To sing such a melody that lifts up the soul,
bringing such peace and making us whole.
A song not of words and beautiful speech,
a song that the world finds difficult to teach.

Somewhere inside we find a part,
feeling so deep and sung from the heart.

Worth

Do not look at others to see what you're worth,
searching around from north to south,
asking this person and asking that
if you are too thin or are too fat.

Asking if they see anything in you
that is beautiful and charming, clean and pure.
Seeking recognition, pleading to be seen,
feeling so useless, worthless and mean.

Other's opinions can help or frustrate
the worth you are seeking, so open the gate
to your life and just look at a flower.
It grows so gently and with little power.

It may be diseased and attacked by the wind,
it cannot speak and has no mind,
but still it grows and sways in the breeze
giving it's perfume and beauty in peace.

So learn to see how the flower has grown,
accepting itself for the short life it owns.
Now look at yourself and what do you see,
whatever you are, you're filled with beauty.

Value

The value of a diamond as it sparkles in the sun
and gives of such colour and beauty all round,
or the value of a pearl so smooth and bright,
when set in a necklace, light up the night.
The value of gold so bright and pure,
shining and dazzling with its allure,
or the value of silver when purified in heat,
they all lift up the eyes and away from the feet.
All the gold in the world is worth nothing at all,
compared to a life, so weak and so small.
There are things that money or wealth cannot buy,
a tiny ant, bird or butterfly,
or lion so proud and the skill of a fox,
the eye that can see, the heart that unlocks;
the love from one to another is felt
creating such peace, whatever we're dealt.
So value the things that money can't buy,
the smile on your face will tell you why.

Constant Love

My thoughts may change, with hurt and pain
but my love will always be the same.

Love for my sons or daughter fair,
love even when I do not know where

it comes or goes but one thing is sure;
love that is learned affects rich and poor.

It starts from somewhere deep inside,
if it is true love it will not hide,

but will automatically be shown,
as it is in other lives sown.

I will never stop loving as long as I live
and as long as I have breath, I will give.

The Rocks

The wind blew hard and the sea stirred,
creating a mist made vision blurred.
The waves were angry and frothed and boiled
sailors worked hard as against it they toiled
and life is threatened when tons of water
rise to heights and fill every quarter.
Pounding the beach and tossing the stones,
smashing the concrete and with anxious groans
from many a frightened and terrified man,
seeing the sight preventing his plan.
Stones are thrown against windowpane
as waves mount up in their frame
and floods strike goods and precious things,
which float away as if on wings.
There are many where life has dealt a blow.
When will it end? They do not know.

Look down below from where they climb,
the rocks that stood the test of time
are moving not upon the shore
but standing fast though battered sore.
If in our lives the rocks are built
and battered some, cause us to lilt,
foundation strong will never move,
if laid so firmly it will prove
that things that last are there always
and stay like a rock throughout our days.

Cost

I may lose all my wealth and gold,
or others take and then are sold,
as many reasons loss is there
with failure, doubt and many a care.
I sit and watch as slowly drains
all my inheritance, hard work and strain,
I fell and ground into the dust,
by many others I did trust.
I do not blame, but pity feel,
for those who stamp on with their heel.
When I am empty and undone.
and cannot look and see the sun,
there is one place I always go
and that is upward, without a show
of noise or shouting or attraction
but then it gives me satisfaction,
to know that if I lose my wealth,
and suffer much within my health,
deep inside I know I can try
to reach upward to the sky.

TREASURE WITHIN

The treasure within makes me smile
and makes my living well worthwhile.
Others cannot my treasure find,
the secret's hidden within my mind.
They rush about and store up wealth,
working hard and rich by stealth.
Their mind is used to feed the purse,
and they think they are none the worse
but the reaper comes so silently,
he is not noticed, when turns the key
of life and what we have not done
to give to others the warmth of sun.
The treasure inside me, no one can touch
and rob and spoil very much
because it brings me joy and strength
and will release me again at length.
So when the thief comes to annoy
reach down inside and touch the joy.

EVER LOVE

I will never stop loving you, whatever betide,
whatever is stolen or hurt or pride.

If any pain is ruling still
with anger, revenge or threat to kill.

I cannot help that deep within,
I do not want to hurt or sin.

But when we fall into the dust,
body decay and filled with rust,

something lives on and never lies,
the constant love that never dies.

LITTLE CHILDREN

I remember the times when the children were small,
they played in the garden and sometimes did fall.
I comforted them, disciplined them but always with grace,
always remembering that what they would face
later in life, would be trouble and strife,
maybe some horrible threat to their life.
Remembering that one day, they would bear children too
and have to love them like me and like you.
The lessons they learned would be valuable then,
even though stifled and hidden by men
or cares of this life have snatched them away
of this I am sure that they return one day.
Then they will be good parents of their little ones,
and I will be granddad and watch them in fun.

CRUELTY

Please do not be cruel, what have I done?
What is the purpose to blot out the sun?
Then not content to see me bow low
but hit out with cruel words and actions that flow
from a heart that is hard and hurt deep within,
filled with a hatred and hardened by sin.

Can you not find forgiveness and love?
Is there some glimmer of light from above?
The one who is suffering is not those you strike
with pain and revenge and such a dislike
but if you continue on the course you tread,
deep down inside you, something lies dead.

Fall

Do not be proud and say you can't fall
as there on the hill you are standing so tall,

and working so hard and living your life,
trying to be good and live without strife.

You see someone fall in the distance one day,
as dust and the dirt of the failure to stay

on the course that is set in the great plan of life
has been dealt a blow to him and his wife.

You judge him severely and then you avoid
his path he has trod, with him you're annoyed.

Written off now and thrown out the key
to all that is wholesome, his children not see.

Please do not assume that you cannot fall too,
for if that is so. then the failure is you.

Relationships

Out of doors in the open, looking here and looking there
to the sky, on the ground, deep in thought but anywhere.
People walking, holding hands,
along the street, upon the sand.
Old and young, it matters not
for within the heart it is their lot
to be together from tiny tot
to old woman and man.
Who holds the plan?
Some are large and some are small,
others thin and then some tall,
some have disability and pain
while others have no shelter from rain.

Together long and then some do part,
trembling now with pain of heart.
Others are of different land
but still together, hand in hand.
Looking on, from our dim view
we wonder how their love stays new
but only they know how this is
with arms entwined and lovers kiss.

OLD COUPLE

I walked upon the street one day
as I was going on my way
and as I walked, I noticed there,
crossing the road, an elderly pair.
Both of them had put on weight
as they walked towards their gate.
I watched with interest as they crossed
the road. He was in thought lost,
with cars around, his little wife
hurried to catch up and feared for her life.
She caught him halfway over the road
and then her mind lost its forebode,
because her hand in his she slipped
securely now with his strong grip.

Separation

The pain so deep it can't be told,
warmth has gone and now so cold,
shaking from the fear within,
appetite gone and wasted thin.
Why does this occur to some?
Seeing others having fun
and living life to the full.
Holidays and picnics too,
family, children, skies of blue;
standing lonely, as world goes by
ache inside and tear in the eye.
Lonely one, look to the sky,
and you will be lifted as time passes by.

Accepted

Friends may come and friends may go,
but there is one friend I know.

Loved so much; you seemed always the same,
whenever you spoke you would never blame

but your cheerful smile and friendly wave
opened up hearts and encouragement gave.

I am so glad I knew you and always will miss
your acceptance of everyone. Now I know this

that our lives are enriched whenever we find
a good friend like you so willing and kind.

I will never forget you, the times were so few
that I enjoyed your company and your friendship too.

New Life

You may have wandered far and wide
and sought for pleasure, vanity and pride,
then longing more for earthly gain
you plunder, lust and push through rain
until you feel the aching void
inside so deep it cries aloud.
Your mind, it groans with pain and hurt
as body racked and so inert,
searching, searching many paths,
satisfaction far from your grasp;
until one day, when sinking down
upon earth's bed, with a frown,
so low now into the dust.
Why is life so unjust?
The years have gone and wasted now,
as on your knees, with body bowed,
tiredness envelopes every thought.
Is this the life that I have bought?
Purposeless and meaningless,
was I born just for this?
"Never" was the whisper heard
and deep inside something stirred,
like waking from a silent sleep.
Realisation, I will not keep
those things that caused me stumble blind,
in letting go, only then will find
the peace of heart and soul and mind
and healing balm that comes so kind,
enveloping all and giving new strength,
as God's good grace does come at length,
giving new life, when death has done
its worse, in blotting out the sun.
There is no more that it can do,
we rise, as making all things new.

Eyes

I saw a man stood on a mound,
staring hard upon the ground,
and wondered why he stood so still,
was he paralysed or ill?
I saw him lift his eyes at last
and stared at mine an icy blast,
something hard and piercing cold
deep inside his mind and soul.

I slowly turned my gaze away
and saw the trees and sunlit day,
looking up, I saw the sky
with clouds that drifted slowly by.
I glanced about and saw the sea
so blue and sparkling brilliantly,
the fun as little children play,
their shrieks of laughter fill the day.

I hesitate, slowly as I would
to see the mound where he had stood.
Now he had gone. My thoughts at last
wondered why the icy blast
had risen from his heart so cold
and if he spoke, his story told
might be of deep and anguished pain
of unhealed hurt and full of blame,
perhaps had sunk into the mire
of darkened thoughts, not able to aspire
to higher things as sunshine and breeze,
lofty mountains and swaying trees,
seaside sounds and family fun.
Where had he gone? Away from the sun.

RULING

There are some that rule with open mind
and peace of heart and words so kind,

giving generously from what they have
to those that are hungry, poor or a slave.

They rule with justice and full of truth,
aspiring others to have goodness and faith.

Their authority is earned and humbly used,
while others take and rule with abuse,

dominating and ruling with iron,
scorning the weak, to tread upon.

Climbing to heights not earned or given,
to satisfy selfishness and ambition.

In climbing the ladder of success and achieve
those who are broken and battered they leave.

Remember, when placed in authority
over others, to rule with humility.

Do not abuse the lives in your care,
in ruling them, let them see you are fair.

NAKED

He hid in the doorways so naked and torn
many that saw him, laughed him to scorn.

Huddled in the corner. robbed of all wealth,
coughing and groaning and lacking in health.

"Disgusting" said some and another a coin
tossed to him it rolled and fell down a drain.

Now the young man shed a tear, which left streaks
down his pale face so dirty and bleak,

all his clothes one did steal while he slept,
now left with nothing he silently wept.

He remembered the day he left his home,
an angry outburst from his father had come

because he committed an unholy crime,
thrown from his house for the passing of time.

Judged by the good and the clean living ones,
as well as the evil and abusers of sons.

An elderly woman passed by that street
glancing his way and seeing unshod feet,

shuffled up to him and took off her coat
to cover his nakedness, her scarf round his throat.

Those that passed by thought she was a fool
to take such a chance and act like a mule,

she could have been robbed and then lay half dead,
tending that dirty young man that had bled

by the side of the road, filled with filth and disease
but filled with her gentleness, love and her peace

she did not condemn him but played her part
for her actions had come from a mother's heart.

CONDEMNATION

"Condemn him" they shouted, "and lock him inside,
throw out the key, his sin will not hide.
How could he do such a thing as this?"
Picking up stones to hurl and not miss.

"Take him away from family and friends,
even if he changes and tries to make amends,
we will never forgive him but condemn him to die,
making him suffer and sink, by and by."

Just then, a stranger passed by that way
and seeing the commotion there, on that day,
he stood still and erect between condemned and the crowd,
as they cursed and swore and shouted out loud.

"Stop", said the stranger, "take me instead,
I've had a good life and if I am dead,
then this man can live and do wrong no more,
with forgiveness and love and feeding the poor."

The crowd was so angry but reluctantly agreed,
the condemned man hurried away for now he was freed
and turning around he saw the crowd run
straight at the stranger until he was done.
He sank to his knees and wept 'til he was sore,
at this stranger's sacrifice, as he was no more.

Disabled

It may be the limbs or voice or mind,
the life now lived is cruel and unkind,
time passes by so slowly now
the heart is pained and furrowed brow.

Inner thoughts cause tears to fall
upon the ground. No one hears the call
from deep within and nobody sees
within the mind, like they can; the trees.

Sometimes the pain is unseen and long,
stirring the heart and silence the song.
Through no fault of our own we're dealt a blow
or maybe we wrong someone we know

but whatever the reason, the pain's still the same,
some feel the pity, others the blame.
The cry of the heart ascending from earth
from millions of sufferers, the old and at birth.

Can you not feel it ascending on high?
From those that are weary and preparing to die,
From some life has drained but heart still beats on,
spare them a thought and give them a song.

Give them new hope and life will return,
their soul deep within with fresh faith will burn.
Never despise them, a smile has no cost
but it has such a benefit in reaching the lost.

SELF

Going to church or doing good deeds
rooting out wrong and digging up weeds,
honest to all we smile to ourselves
forgetting that some are left on the shelf.
That shelf of their loneliness and poverty great
body so dirty and mind in a state.
No one to help them and no one to call
or lift them on high from where they did fall.

Many pass by and live their own life,
having a family, marry a wife,
job so secure and comforts at home,
sparing no thought for those that do roam,

with no place to rest and nowhere to sleep
wandering around, just like lost sheep.
Relax in your riches you feel you have earned
remembering this, that the tables may turn.

SHAME

There in the corner, just by the wall
stood a young man, now not so tall,
with head that was bowed and hands that shook,
remembering with shame the things that he took.

Why was he so foolish? It raced through his mind.
Clock cannot turn back, men not so kind,
pointing the finger with accusing so cruel,
fire burns within and flamed with such fuel.

His head now hangs lower and tears start to fall,
friends all have left him, not one he can call.
The tears now are burning on cheek and fall down,
he remembered his dreams of earning a crown.

Many years passed by since that early dream
of life with such honour, in his early teens.
Family have left him, such shame could not bear,
why is there no one will stand with him there?

Then one came alongside him, midst taunts from nearby
"I will stand with you, for I now know why
you fell in disgrace and the shame that you bear,
I have felt too and now I can share

in another's disgrace, for I have climbed out
of the state I was in, of that there's no doubt."
The stranger he put his arm gently around
the waist of the young man with eyes on the ground

and slowly he realised that someone that cared,
someone still loved him and willing to share.
His eyes now so moist from the hot burning tears
and dirty and bloodshot from crying in fear.

A smile now appeared, though so small at the first
as slowly the realisation in his heart did burst.
"All that I needed was a friend by my side
to carry my burden of shame I can't hide.
Can I believe that with me you will stay?
when all of my other friends have run away.
Please do not leave me, hold me so close,
so sorry I am dirty from head to my toes.

Oh, to feel clean again, please help me friend,
then I can start living and then make amends."

Together

We all stand together like it or not
living in this world, in our small slot.

No independence or standing alone,
heart that is kind or set like a stone.

We breathe the same air and walk the same road
through life, until death brings its heavy load.

While we are here, do not fight and accuse,
suffering and hurting and giving abuse.

Live with each other as brothers and friends
giving out love, prepared to bend,

in humility and service, enriching their lives,
put down the spears and away with the knives.

Only through forgiveness to those who have wronged
our hearts will be lighter, a beautiful song.

Discipline

A parent exasperated, standing in a shop,
tired, so tired and fit to drop.
the child is crying and screaming aloud,
embarrassed, embarrassed among the crowd.

The rules that are made when the noises stop
have little place in the crowded shop.
In anger the parent strikes the noisy child.
Why are they naughty and being so wild?

A tear falls now upon the parent's face,
the rule that they made is broken in a trice,
the shocked child, hurt and stunned in pain,
falls silent now, looks at parent with blame.

This would not happen in quiet of home,
to discipline in anger would not be known,
discipline then, for motive bad
was what they knew and what they had.

Strange, how when we grow up fast
and stand so tall, a man at last
and when we fail and fall away,
we're thrown in prison for night and day.

The punishment for actions done,
hidden away and locked out the sun.
Where is the help for motives bad?
To change the man from being sad
and bring release to give again
and make amends to fellow men.

SEARCHING

Search among the rubbish pile
over fields and under stile,
look at faces feeling sad,
losing all the joy they had.
Live our lives and walk on by
do not see the misty eye;
just ignore the pile of rags
in a heap by rubbish sacks
but look again, there lays a man
who loses all, the world has banned,
he has no hope but waits to die.
Will you leave him? Let him lie?
'Don't get involved' the call comes loud,
will you walk with rest of crowd?
Or stand alone and lift him out,
with little thanks, there's no doubt,
but you will know you've done your best
and lay at night in bed to rest
with peaceful sleep and calm of heart,
knowing that you played your part.
Don't ignore the sick and lost,
help them now whatever cost,
search the places now they hide
in shame and loneliness abide.
Lift them up to face the light,
make their darkness out of sight.

Missed Truth

Look at the splendid mountains so large
or the stars in the sky, or lightening charge.
See the morning mist and sunset sky,
the earth so green or clouds that fly.

Maybe we notice the tallest trees
or rushing wind and gentle breeze,
or the wonder of birth with a perfect child
or storm lashed rocks with sea so wild.

The fury of a whirlwind or tornadoes power
causing many strong men to hide and cower.
There are many mighty and powerful things
like the swiftest horse or eagles wings

but some things not noticed and often passed by
such as the smallest ant or tiny fly,
or maybe the bird singing in the tree
or worm underground or tiny flea.

A world exists in the tiniest things,
so easily crushed and the truth it brings.

True Riches

Rattle the collecting box, "give to the poor".
This was the cry from door to door.
Some were so wealthy and made a great show,
much in the box they placed, faces a glow.

Upper class, middle class, lower class too
all were invited many and few.
Knocking on doors and pleading for more,
'til one old woman, they knocked on her door.

Shuffling, hobbling with her old stick,
she came to the door. Could not be quick

but slowly the door opened and two tiny coins
were dropped in the box with little noise.

The door closed again and she went back in
the collector noticed and said with a grin,
"is that all she could manage? Surely some more,
like the others have given from their own store!"

What he did not know is she gave all she had,
and inside was hungry but never sad,
for she had discovered the source of true wealth
is only in giving, true peace she now felt.

Others had given out of a full purse
and what they had left was none the worse.
The secret is giving with nothing to give,
out of a pure heart, that others might live.

Hypocrisy

A thousand words and many good deeds,
good wishes and thoughts but are there weeds?
The weeds of unreality bind and choke
the life of beauty, its roots they soak
with poison and bitterness, affecting the flower
that struggles to bloom in the right hour.
The flower bursts through but withers and dies
before its beauty is seen by the eyes,
we all have such beauty inside our shell,
why let hypocrisy make it like hell?
Be honest and real with our fellow man
if feeling low or depressed, don't be a sham
but speak from sincerity and a pure heart
others will welcome an honest part.
Fear of rejection is often the cause
Just when the words are there, making us pause
but don't be afraid for we are the same
just for defence will cause us to blame.
Take courage and say what is real on your heart
with kindness and gentleness and play your part.

Change

We all need change whatever the age
whatever our circumstance, locked in a cage,
if high on a mountain top or deep in the sea
feeling that nobody can ever touch me.

Changing is good and can bring a fresh view
making us stand and making us new.
Submit to the changes that bring us distress
and cause us to think we're in a deep mess.

Even when things are good and roses in bloom,
always remember there must be some room
for constant change and the fresh air it brings
with a reminder, don't hang onto things.

Things come and go and turn into dust,
travel to new places for change is a must.

Worry

Why do you worry and panic so?
Why do you fret and fear tomorrow?
Will it change one inch of your life?
Change circumstance or rid us of strife?
Face up to trouble and with trembling hands
and troubled heart, make our stand,
and whatever the outcome, we have done our best,
able to lie down, sleep and to rest
without disturbance of worry and fret,
satisfied now that our troubles we met.

Intimacy

Intimacy brings pleasure but sometimes brings pain
many get hurt but we dare not refrain
from being close to others and the joy that it brings,
bringing out melody, causing to sing.
The closer we are the more we get hurt,
pain deep inside, cleans out the dirt
of security, pride and all that offends,

bringing humility and makes us to bend
into serving another with deep love and trust,
seeing each fault turn into dust.
We cling to each other in loving embrace,
whatever our creed or gender or race,
forgiving so freely and pressing on
forward until the race is won.

FAILURE

Down the town, into the shops,
the smile that comes and never stops.
Chatting and laughing and meeting others
never a hint of any bother.

The elderly man with stick in his hand
shuffled along, so cheerful a stand.
Passers by thought he'd no care in the world
but he was hiding a heart that felt cold.

As he arrived at his small town flat,
took off his coat and hung up his hat,
such a long sigh came from deep down inside,
no time to laugh now and no room for pride.

He remembered when young and filled up with pride
he foolishly robbed and someone had died.
He spent years in prison and never forgot
the old man in the shop, the person he shot.

If he could live again, he'd make things anew
and not be so foolish but have a fresh view,
he's now served his time and an old man himself,
never was married and left on the shelf.

Why did I waste my life, he thought again,
for one stupid action, shut away from friends,
I've learned my lesson, for this life, too late,
one day, for the last time, I'll pass through the gate,

I'll meet my Maker and what will he say?
Forgiveness is everything and brings a new day.

Flame

Flame burning brightly, shatters the night,
with its deep darkness, terror and fright.
Light overcomes the darkness we dread,
giving new life to what was once dead.

Whether a flicker or blazing fire
is the light that we burn, it will not tire
to bring some new comfort and hope
to those around, struggling to cope.

Strike a match, light a fire, and let it burn bright
stop those whose hearts are cold losing their sight.
Give them new vision of futures untold,
help them rekindle the fire that goes cold,
do not give up on them and let bitterness reign,
light a blaze and fan the flame.

Destiny

A plan mapped out, written in ink,
causing to ponder, making us think.
Right or wrong, left or right,
where is the path? Give us the light.

Look straight ahead, seeing the goal,
never let anything shatter our soul.
Guarding our heart with passions aflame,
do not let others have someone to blame.

Sometimes walking and then we run
when clouds are hiding the brightness of sun.
Keep pressing forward, eyes open wide
missing nothing and nothing to hide,
then we will reach our goal, planned in advance,
grasping all that is ours, leave nothing to chance.

Who Am I?

Wander around, turn this way and that,
discovering life at the drop of a hat,
growing through childhood and then through teens,
things are so new and not what they seem.

Life is discovery that comes with each day,
grow and look forward in our special way.
Unique, individual, all not the same,
others have travelled, not the way we came.

We live on this earth and the pathway we tread
is ours and no one can stand in our stead.
Although there are millions who walk on the road,
some carry emptiness, while others a load.

We're here for each other and not walk alone,
holding up those who fall, carry them home.
Only when functioning for them in this way,
will we discover our part we play.

FORGIVENESS

A young man, full of exuberant youth,
went with a crowd, language uncouth,
exciting, thrilling, zeal and such fun,
better than being alone as one.

Looking forward every day
to hearing all his friends say,
with pat on the back and smiling face,
"how brave you are and handsome face."

He went to the gym and built up his strength,
his ego rose and took over at length,
surrounded by those who saw he could lead,
powerful and strong, knowing no need.

Eventually, his ego went down a path,
blinded, stumbling along in the dark,
'til one day encouraged to break in and steal
some jewellery to sell and buy a nice meal.

As he was creeping through the large house,
silently, stealthily, like a small mouse,
the owner surprised him and challenged his right
to be there and trespass in middle of night.

Frightened and stronger, the young man struck
the owner and killed him. A piece of bad luck,
he thought, as he ran and hid from the law
and left the owner's wife and children so poor.

The wife was so hurt, her heart could not mend,
for the young man had stolen her dearest friend.
At length, the young man was caught and thrown
in prison, with sentence and he was disowned,

by family and friends who left him to rot,
locked away, for him they cared not.
In time, the wife who felt so lonely and sad,
wrote to the man, who robbed children of Dad,

The Mist of Yesterday

and said she forgave him for his past deed,
and wanted to help him to pull out the weeds
of his life that had caused him to steal and to hurt
innocent victims. He knelt in the dirt,

of his cell and cried when he read
the letter of forgiveness instead.
Not long after, he did die in his cell
of some disease that struck him and made him so ill,

but before he died, he had peace of mind
of knowing the wife that had been so kind.
The hurt may not go when someone is pained
but forgiveness can free a heart that is stained,

by taking wrong paths and failing in life,
see the shining example of this beautiful wife.
The young man had seen in his final hour
that essential forgiveness has a great power,

for if unforgiveness is reigning supreme,
to set someone free, is only a dream,
for though they walk free from prison and chains,
in mind and heart in prison remains.

The Unseen

Lower class, middle and upper too,
some with polite, "How do you do?"
others walk arm in arm and smile as they go,
comfortably relaxed and so much to show.
That others might see the success achieved
on the surface, but underneath, who have they grieved?
Church on a Sunday, cursing unknown,
never a foot wrong, strive for a crown,
eat a balanced diet they say,
and before bed, don't forget to pray.
What is that we see, there by the wall,
a bundle of rubbish; we are appalled
that someone should dump their filthy scrap here
and not in the proper place that is quite near.
Do not go near that dirty place
or you will scrub your hands and face.
To be clean shows holiness they say
and an ordered life, the proper way,
so do not allow the flies and the stench
that comes from that rubbish to cause offence.
They hurry on by and hope that they have
not been contaminated or damaged their faith
by looking upon such empty waste,
right in the mouth it leaves a bad taste.
What no one noticed that this was the home
of someone with nothing and destined to roam,
for he had offended and brought himself low
with nothing but shame was all he could show.
Therefore he hid in the bags of such dirt,
hoping he'd not be seen without a shirt
but only the rags that for years he had worn,
some were so filthy, and others were torn.
Sitting there deep in thought he pondered why,

but still did not blame them for passing him by,
family and friends had long gone their way
and forgotten he existed, as they went to pray.
He had offended and hurt them he knew
and sighed with deep regret, not just a few.
Just then a poor man shuffling by
looked down upon him and started to cry,
for he had nothing to give this lost soul,
nothing to help him and make him feel whole.
He wiped his tears dry and gazed on the man,
who turned his face away and looked at the sand,
the poor stranger sat down with a welcoming smile,
'I cannot give wealth or food by the pile,
or anything others would think of as good
and benefit to them, as shun me they would
but something I can give, which is worth more than wealth,
I can give you encouragement and give you myself'.

Bitter

"Never forgive, stand your ground'
the call received from far around.
Revenge is sweet, or so they say,
make them suffer, make them pay
for all the wrong and lousy ways
they made you suffer in past days.
it does not matter that they regret
the way they were since first you met.
Many counsellors, much advice,
some is good, some not so nice.
Confusion reigns, head in a spin,
'what do I do, will I ever win?'.
Satisfaction must be found
and stop this turning round and round.
You once were young but now grow old,
before the complete tale is told.
You once did laugh and sing with joy
but now the smallest thing annoys.
"See how I suffer', the cry is heard,
the air is still the silent birds.
There is only one way to bring release
and turn your torment into peace.
Do not listen to those who cry,
'make them suffer, then to die!',
but listen to your heartbeat deep inside
and swallow every ounce of pride.
Then forgive and embrace the pain,
lift from another the very stain
and reason for what was lost,
lay down the sword and count the cost.
The thing we fear will vanish then,
dry the tears and stop the rain,
the sun will shine and chase the night
and make an impossible future bright.

Running

Do not run in fear and hide
and shake and tremble from inside,
when all around seems big and tall
and you seem insignificant and small.

The more you run and not face the foe,
with lack of confidence, so the enemy grows,
a hill is a mountain, impossible to cross,
never enough to meet the cost.

It is only when we turn and stand
our ground and face the task at hand
and then advance upon the host
we gain the ground we thought was lost,
and then we feel new courage found,
breaking the cords that we were bound.

Recognition

Must we be thanked for all that we do?
All that we say for comfort true?
We give our money, time and toil
to help another and turn the soil.
As we look around and see others smile
with thanks, it all seems so worthwhile.
We feel so good and warm inside,
pleased with ourselves and a little pride
starts to erupt and struggles begin,
the pride takes over, becomes a sin.
What starts with encouragement can be so lost,
happiness goes, we count the cost.
Therefore the question comes to mind,
'does too much recognition make us blind
to what is important in this life,
like peace inside, instead of strife?'
Many do give of all they have
but never thanked for what they gave.
The satisfaction and smile on their face
tells the story of a life rich with grace.

The Vagrants

I parked my car in the usual place,
life was so busy, hurry and haste.
I locked it and checked it and started to walk
to my place of business to do my work.

I felt uneasy as I walked away
from my car, so clean on that summers day.
For there, on the wall two old men sat,
one was thin and one was fat.

They were singing a song and filled with beer,
no one would venture too near, through fear.
I worried for my car, my pride and joy,
for me it was my little toy,

but as I walked away and glanced back
and saw the clothes that they did lack
and dirty face and hands of grime
and wondered what had been their crime

to bring them to a place as this.
I wondered would their family miss
their company, or are they written off
from this world's society so aloft.

I felt some shame that I took a part
in judging them from in my heart,
when fearing they might damage my car,
when drink took over, went too far.

I determined more that I would care
for those unfortunate, worse for wear,
no matter what it cost my way
for maybe that is me some day.

Dreams

Shut in behind bolted door,
whether we're rich or whether poor,
in lands far away across the sea,
away from loved ones or family.

Riding the ocean as sailors do,
a lonely life and friends are few,
food is scarce, the pain of drought,
little water and mind filled with doubt.

Faith is lost, to what purpose life?
Never a hope of gaining a wife
and children. So nothing new,
or costly gain and debts are due.

Is this our lot, as we lay down
without a bed upon the ground?
Whatever happens in battered life,
like waves upon the rocks of strife,

we dream and gently sink into
another world of green and blue.
A world that rises from the dust
and lifts our spirit, give us trust

and faith once more when we arise
from sleep of beauty to our eyes.
The world of dreams will bring a smile
and make our life so much worth while,

for we have flown to far off lands
and gently walked across the sand
and gazed upon the ocean blue,
wondering why we feel so new.

This dream, no one can snatch away,
for in our mind is there to stay.

SEASONS

Winter, summer, autumn, spring,
as seasons change, new songs we sing,
a song of laughter, sadness too,
songs that come when thoughts are few.
One day sunshine, then comes the rain,
days of happiness, then of pain.
The winter covers what was living,
now back into the ground is giving,
to raise again, new life in spring
fills the earth, the heart will sing,
with warmth of summer's sun and breeze,
and golden showers and swaying trees.
Perfumed beauty all around
lift our eyes from off the ground,
for seasons of life that come and go,
they all are important for us to grow.

AMBITION

A hurried kiss, a quick goodbye,
the wife, she waves, as husband cries
about his lateness by and by.
Surrounded now, by those rich friends,
that come for dinner and they blend
into surroundings meant for those
of wealth and power, jewellery glows,
admiring glances, envying greet
from those who struggle to make ends meet
and feel that life is just not fair,
with body sign of wear and tear
but no one sees the harm that hides
deep within ambition's pride.
The doorbell rings, the wife now goes
to answer it, face all aglow
but when she sees the police are there,

suddenly she feels the care.
Her husband rushed so quick to work,
for profit, now he could not shirk.
He felt a pain within his chest,
sweat was pouring from his breast.
He swerved and crashed his car into
a tree and then a flashing light of blue,
as ambulance came, took him away
for many months of rest, that day.
Thankful now for life was spared
and grateful for a wife that cared,
he changed his life, as it was clear
ambition then had cost him dear.
Ambition now and friends among
the lonely, poor and those who clung
to life of failure; gave them hope,
the will to live and power to cope.

My Personal Friend

No matter what I have done or where I have been
I have a friend that no one has seen.
He is powerful, unreachable to those who in pride
hang onto ugliness deep down inside.
Life is a mess, mistakes have been made.
Is there an answer? Why have I stayed
here in the gloom, bemoaning my lot,
wandering around, stumbling and not
opening my eyes to the real truth within.
Truth that can conquer, truth that can win.
Truth that gives hope to a lost dying world,
hope of a future, new plans unfurled.
This friend will forgive and we will feel clean,
no matter what we have done or where we have been.
Silence the voices that call and condemn
and listen instead to my dearest friend.

POWER

Power is so dangerous, if not handled right,
power can ignore or strike in the night.
Power can control or manipulate those
who in weakness and fear cannot oppose.

Some do not recognise the power they wield
but think they are giving advice and a shield
to those who are weaker and often fall,
stumbling around and feeling so small.

Remember that true power will always have grace
to give out to those who have not a face
in this world of greed and lusting to win
by those climbing ladders, treading on kin.

"Get there at all costs", the cry that we hear,
ignoring the ones that are living in fear.
Power thus used will quickly fade
and sink to oblivion the world we have made

for ourselves, when we reach the pinnacle of fame,
pointing the finger, to others we blame.
The power of wealth, the power to rule,
power to buy the world's greatest jewel.

All will be nothing in the final defeat
of the top of the castle, our great retreat.
So use power wisely, if this is our gift,
encouraging those that in weakness do shift

from one road to another in pursuit of their goal,
feeling so empty with a need to be whole.
Then at the last satisfaction will reign
knowing our power has given others the gain.

Win

The runners kept their eye on the goal,
as they waited at the start to be told
to commence the race. Then they were off,
but this race was not for the soft
or the weak of heart or frame,
or those without a name.
The crowd roared and cheered,
the track had been cleared,
there was nothing in the way
on that fine sunny day.
Finally the race was won
by the strongest, somebody's son.
Parents proud, cheered out loud
standing there among the crowd,
did not notice someone was last
looking lonely and downcast.
Then I saw another race
but there were those that without face
or important name, for they were lame,
this race was not the same
but wheelchairs raced and the crowd roared,
the winner here had broke the cord.
Not one competitor retired in shame
but congratulated for playing the game.

Alone

"Why be alone?' 'Make some new friends'
this is the cry that others did send,
not understanding his loneliness felt
deep down inside his heart that will melt.
The pain is so real, with aching inside,
thoughts of the past he cannot hide,
even though finding new friends that surround,
lifting his eyes and face from the ground,
no one can heal the ache of the heart
that constantly lingers, while he played a part.
Then when he shut the door once again,
alone in his room and thankful for friends,
he lay on his bed and thoughts drift away
to times in the past in some distant day,
when he walked with his wife along the seashore,
talking together, although they were poor
did not seem to matter for hand in hand then
he walked with his wife, his loveliest friend.
Now left with memories in the quiet of his mind
of the love that he shared with the wife so kind,
a tear fell down, for now she was gone
and he is now left so quiet and alone.
The blame has long gone and guilt has all passed
for his failure in life, his soul peace at last.
Torn hearts that heal will always be scarred
lives have been changed when in this way they're marred.
Slowly a smile spreads across his lined face,
as he thought of her charm and of her sweet grace
and knowing with faith he'll meet her again
and then in that moment heal silent pain.

Dad

I remember when I was a young boy
you were strict and I was annoyed
and resentful of the way you acted
as upon my life it was impacted.
Then gradually, as the years went by,
there emerges another cry;
hearts that ached and tears were shed,
we made mistakes, down paths were led.
I slowly realised you did your best,
although you hurt inside your chest,
I know that all the while did seek
for something that you could not reach.
As I look back upon your life,
you lost a child and then a wife,
things were not easy but I am glad
that with your new wife the joy you had,
will always live on in memory still,
as life goes on with us until
we meet again where you are gone,
enjoying friends and long lost son.
Dear Dad I miss you, miss your hug,
miss your humour, sense of fun.
It's strange but only when you're gone,
the ache I feel inside is strong.

Feelings

Stifle true feelings, put on a brave face,
this is the cry with many a race,
the hardness around in hearts that have lost
the art of compassion. We counted the cost,
not wanting to pay for love that will change
our selfish ambition and running from pain.

Hurting and pain must not once be named
in our busy lifestyle with fun and a game,
but one day when lonely and all by ourselves
the tears of our feelings will stay where they fell.
Do not run and hide from the pain that you feel,
experience it's changing, your mind it will heal.

New Life

Just like a chrysalis alone in the ground,
silent and still, cannot be found,
'til warmth of the sun upon the cold earth,
something is stirring and bringing new birth.

Struggling, straining and gaining new strength,
a beautiful creature emerges at length.
Bursting forth into a new day,
stretching stiff wings and flying away.

Higher and higher into the bright sky,
struggles now over a new butterfly.
Mistakes that are made in roads that we tread,
regrets, disappointments, so much is said
but look at the positive, beautiful end
and the tale of our lives becomes a firm friend.

Saying goodbye will last just a while,
l remember in my mind just seeing your smile.
That is one picture I'll never forget,
there at the window, when last time we met.

Live On

When someone dies then life goes on,
memories linger, for a while without sun,
hearts and minds that ache inside,
privately grieving thoughts to hide.

No one knows the pain that is felt
from those who loved. The cards are dealt,
whatever our lot in life we see,
mistakes are made but we hold the key

to turn the tide, bring something new
out of this dying, new life pursue.
Love, forgiveness a change of heart
to those that live on in playing their part.

Over

Now it is over, the relatives are gone,
tears have been shed, you lay beneath the sun,
buried now, with flowers on your grave.
Where are you? What is there to save?
We stood there watching, as you were lowered down,
by strong cords, down into the ground.
As I watched, silent in my grief,
thoughts now racing. Death is such a thief,
parting those who love and care, tossing hearts aside,
and even as I'm standing there, inside I run to hide.
So much taken from without but things we cannot see,
something stirs from deep within for now we can be free.
Free from pain and aching hearts when we stand alone
for only then can we find that hearts unite as one.
A hug, a kiss, an arm around a trembling, shaking chest,
reminding us that there are those that live their very best,
encouraging and sharing, moving silently around,
wishing not to be noticed; this is where they're found.
Even though you hurt inside, it's when you look around,
you see a lonely, tired life, with eyes fixed on the ground.
It may be over, some may think, for love have passed away
but not for us with hearts that feel and long to give that way.

My Friend

So quiet, mind is numb and heart that feels so still.
Am I alive and well or do I feel so ill?
I have been so long alone, I do not really know,
if I have passed a certain point. Do I really have to grow?

I look outside upon the grass and see the gentle breeze,
the sun is shining now and leaves are on the trees.
Flowers are blooming, full of colour; smell is in the air,
as I gaze into the sunlight, sat upon my chair.

How did I feel several months ago?
So much has happened, so much to know,
but there are some things I regret,
things that make me so ashamed and long to forget.

Now I am quiet and feel the silence, noise is far away,
the things that inside I feel are with me to stay.
What has taken place before is now a distant past,
I know and feel inside, for peace has come at last;

the peace for which I longed and yearned,
'tis something that I could not earn,
so silently and still did send,
that peace given to me by my friend.

This friend that never let me go,
although my life had little to show,
or so I felt with eyes looked in
to heart so heavy, full of sin

but this forgiving, gentle one,
lifted my head to see the sun.
As I slowly lifted my gaze,
I saw his eyes, through the haze.

Things now clearing and then I gasped,
the love I saw, I had not grasped,
I thought I knew but I was blind
of love that reached into my mind.

The Mist of Yesterday

He never condemned, forgiveness flowed
from one whose life had always showed
such gentleness and purity to teach,
for which I longed and could not reach.

If only I could be like him,
full of love, no trace of sin,
I turned, saw my reflected face,
eyes now wet and tears that traced

on cheeks so scarred and torn with pain
and failure, when all I wanted in my life
was to please this friend, without the strife.
Now I sit alone at last,
yet not alone; my friend has cast

his shadow right across my way,
that where I tread will bring new day.

Debt

What is that shadow in your eyes?
Can you not lift your head to the skies?
You started so well and life was good,
filled with laughter, where you stood.

I now see a tear on your cheek,
you have lost the will to seek
for something better within your life,
as you share it with your wife.

With shoulders hunched you walk away,
silently you cry and pray.
Your little son holds your hand,
"Daddy, what is it you have planned?"

You stop and look into your little one's eyes,
"Don't worry Daddy, I'll look after you", he cries.
Now the tears fall down to the ground,
as he looked up and heard a sound.

"My little darling, Daddy's failed you so much,
I have nothing to give but only my touch,
I am so sorry, little one,
nothing to give you, so you can have fun"

The answer comes as his little face
gazed into only one place
and as he looked into your eyes,
he said, which took you by surprise,

"I only want you Daddy, hold my hand, so
please hold me tight and don't let me go"
Life's more important than silver and gold,
what we own or what we hold.

Tomorrow can bring a better day,
as you climb up that ladder, come what may,
holding each other with encouragement and grace,
gazing with honesty into each other's face.

Riches will come but they can also go,
so hold on loosely to whatever you show.
We all can slide the slippery slope
of debt that leaves us without hope,
so never judge another who falls
but lift him up, so he can stand tall.

Lessons

The lessons of life are hard to bear,
as we watch another filled with care
and know what it feels like, with pain within
as we look back and remember the sin.

A cry on our shoulder tears us apart
and deep inside, pulls at our heart.
When we have walked the way of rocks,
the barrenness, with so many knocks.

We wish we could bear this burden they feel,
as they stumble along, down at heel,
but this is one lesson we cannot bear
as we watch another, so full of care.

We often can give our listening ears
and always be there to dry the tears.

Sadness

It seems to linger for so long,
drains our energy when we were strong,
regrets, the memories of grateful times,
of fun and laughter, as we climbed
the ladder of life, with little care.
Took so much for granted but time was there
and slowly ticking, it passed us by,
youth was spent, success was nigh,
dreams of retirement, relaxing at home,
travelling afar, so much to roam.

The mountain we build is strong as a rock,
it cannot fall as we secure the lock,
sinking back with smile to rest,
the future looks the very best.
Suddenly failure strikes, mistakes are made,
ambition crumbles, future fades
into a mist and as we wildly grasp
the air, as it vanishes, we gasp.

Sweating now, the gold we saved,
the health and life and future craved
has disappeared with questions asked
where we went wrong; we see the past
and hold the embers to our chest;
we thought this was to be the best.

We sink into our sad lost world
of emptiness and useless toil.
Many friends we had have left
us all alone of goods bereft.
Sinking deep into abyss,
grieving, desperate an empty kiss,
but then we see the ground so hard,
life has dealt a cruel card.

The Mist of Yesterday

Our only course, when strength returns,
as sure it will, something burns
within us, just a flicker first,
then a flame, then a burst
of new life and hope from out the dust.
Take one step, of that we must,
then another, stumbling now,
crying, falling, sweating brow.
Persevere through many storms,
then to our surprise, a new day dawns,
we struggle through pain, then to cope;
when there's life, there's always hope.

Emptiness

Once I laughed and life was fun,
feeling loved in warmth of sun;
as a child I played a lot
with other children. Caring not
for trouble, strife and problems too
that came my way. My friendships grew
with school friends, mates and then at work,
I met the ones that I did shirk.
they were unfriendly, some were cruel,
verbal abuse and thought me a fool.
I bravely stood my ground
but slowly inside I found,
my heart that loved and gave to those
in need and lonely, felt the blows
of life with pain, this heart was bruised
but not the way that I did choose.
Down I went and hit the ground,
failing in life, what have I found?
Can I reach up and see the sky?
Can I repair the feelings why?
Is my life over? All I want
is to love others and to plant
in their lives the peace that I have known.
It comes from pain and being alone.
I feel so empty at times but then
I know the pain will come to an end
and I will fly away on wings of peace
emptiness gone, the guilt will cease.
Now I know that deep inside
the joy I feel, I cannot hide;
it comes from loving those in pain
and giving them their joy again.

ADVICE

The young bird sat on the branch in the sun,
he learned to fly and life was so good for this one.
He felt nothing could hurt him or make him afraid
but one day his mother and father had said,
"take care little one when you're flying so high,
the sun is so hot and the danger is nigh".

"My wings are so strong", the youngster had said,
as he took off from the branch, just after he fed.
"To show them", he thought, "they don't understand,
this is the life that for years I had planned".
Higher and higher, up in the cloudless sky,
flapping his wings, felt proud and not tired.

"My parents will watch me and know they were wrong,
with the advice that they gave me, when singing their song".
Everything seemed so small down below,
houses and trees like ants hardly show.
"I feel so hot" he thought as he flew
and suddenly realised, as tiredness grew,
he had not planned for getting back home.

Exhausted he stopped and fell to the earth,
too late he had realised what advice was worth.

My Mind

I remember when I was a boy,
placid and rarely annoyed.
The world seemed so distant and large,
I withdrew into my small cage.

In my little world it was fun,
as I was the only one.
I played by myself,
this world was my wealth,
outside I felt threatened and small,
everyone else seemed so tall.

As I increased in my age,
life still goes on, page by page.
Like a bird thrown out of the nest,
my parents thought they knew best
and opened the rusty cage door,
I stumbled out, fell to the floor.

The sun burned my eyes
and then I realised
as my toys fell away
and I wanted to stay
in the warmth of my little cage.
Now I am grown and my age
has increased but so has the pain
of learning through sunshine and rain.

The joy I have found in my life
has come through having a wife.
Then children were born
and married their own,
with grandchildren come into the frame.
I made mistakes and soiled my family name,
now I am alone, a man without home,
the terrible price for our wrong
brings pain and hurt which is long.

The Mist of Yesterday

When will it end?
A man without friend
is impossible to exist in this world,
yet some still go on in their soiled
and stained life, carry on all alone.

Burst out of the cage we have made,
take courage and strength, do not fade
into the dark mist that others have placed
in your path. You must face
your destiny and goal, look ahead
the dirt and the guilt you must shed.

Do not look back but straight on,
you may stumble but run; face the sun,
let it's brilliance dazzle your eyes,
shake off the cage and its ties,
live life to the full and breathe air,
walk forward without any care,
sun will shine again as you find a friend,
life that is broken will mend.

Gentle

Be gentle with one another,
your sister or brother
or just a colleague or friend
or somebody you send
a letter or card or just a smile,
it makes their living well worth while.

Aggressiveness will never win,
nor will anger, mixed with sin.
Communicate your thoughts and feelings
and careful when you have your dealings
with those whose hearts are tender and bruised
from others that strike and choose
to wound and hurt for selfish end,
losing brothers or faithful friends.

Next time you meet a lonely heart,
seek their welfare, play your part,
bind the wounds with hands that care
not for self or gaining there
but only to enrich another life,
with reason to live, away from strife.
Whatever is given is reaped again,
when you discover you've found a friend.

Worth

You were abused by your father, when young,
he was cruel to you and his words, they stung,
pretending to love you, he loved himself,
from the age of eight, he damaged your health.

Now you are thirty, the brush has been tarred,
suffering ill-health, psychologically scarred,
you cannot cry, so angry you feel,
is there an answer? Can you be healed?

You went down a road into shame and disgrace,
conscience so damaged as you hung your face,
then went into drugs and sexual thrills,
you wasted away and looked very ill.

Then one day I met you and hugged you so tight,
when others rejected you, lost in the night.
I saw the gold in you, which sparkled within
and shone through your wasted body, laden with sin.

Lift up your eyes and look into mine,
see there the gentleness, let your face shine.
As I look into your eyes full of fun,
eyes that are blue and shine as the sun,

I see the sadness of past hurt and shame,
you hide it so well, you were on the game.
Look so much deeper and let it all go,
see the gold inside you and as it flows,
you will be amazed as your worth is what you see
for you are so beautiful and radiant to me.

The Game Of Life

Life is a game of throwing a dice,
given one chance or maybe twice,
or many times dealt the same hand
but eventually what is planned
will return to face us fair and square,
if we are here or maybe there.

Whatever we are and whatever we do
our words and deeds returning true,
what we sow we reap in another way,
in actions and deeds and what we say,
whether by gentle touch or sleight of hand,
deceit or anger, the sinking sand

of time will tell as clock ticks on
and never still. We have our fun
but the years gone by
cannot return to be changed; why
do we think the past cannot affect
the present, future, the written text?

How we live today in the game of life
can affect the future and cut like a knife
through past mistakes, regrets and tears
and all the wasted earlier years.

So be kind to all, forgiving and strong,
never judge and holding no wrong
against another, for they will walk too
on this journey of life, with years all too few.

Mistakes

You made mistakes but I loved you still;
cared for you healthy and when you were ill.
Nothing you do can ever quench love
that holds you and grips you with strength from above.
You went far away from all that is clean
and beautiful, lovely and what was seen
was emptiness, blindness, hurt and despair,
im misty darkness and empty stare.
I do not ask why or judging stance,
remembering that I, with just a glance
can fall from grace and everything good
in just the same way and be misunderstood.
We row the same boat as we travel along,
if I can help you or bring you a song,
give a kind word, forgive you your wrong,
hold you up from the dust of defeat,
no blame but challenging not to repeat
the mistakes you have made as you stumbled along,
now it is different, bring right out of wrong.

Feelings

Mixed up feelings — my head's in a spin;
will I lose or will I win?
Spinning round and back again,
Will someone help me — be my friend?

Knowing myself is hard to find,
who am I? Body and mind?
I only want to love and give
of myself that others live,

but I have to realise I have needs too,
so much for me and so much for you.
Confusion reigns — what do I hear?
In my head, I cannot bear.

So many voices, well meaning ones
but they are loud and fast; clouds and not sun.
Tears are flowing thick and fast,
will I find my peace at last?

Friends are failing and leave me alone,
I sit aside and inward groan.
Shut out the voices and listen to one
deep in your heart, it's gentle tone

will still your soul and bring you peace,
noise abating and turmoil cease.
Loneliness will last awhile
then you will emerge and give a smile.

Confidence will make you strong
when you have the peace for which you long.
So listen to the whispering of inner soul
that comes so quietly and makes you whole,
and you will finally find at length
that in quietness and confidence will be your strength.

INSECURITY

I found a friend and love to be
near him and feeling free
but when he's not there
I am frightened and scared
that friendship will cease
and I will lose my peace.
Be secure within and do not strive
to hold a friendship but let it live
and run it's course so naturally,
then be anxious not but feeling free.
Let others live their lives
and wanting then to give
instead of taking for yourself
will keep your friendship in good health.

DISCOVERING

To find out the truth; what happens next?
My mind in a whirl; my spirit is vexed.
Thoughts that are racing; the hands by my side
are trembling now. I seek to hide
away for a while and think what to do now,
as you were not truthful with me; why and how
I think to myself but slowly it dawns
upon my reasoning. You were a pawn
in the circle of life that effects us all,
when few are chosen but many are called.
When my head now clears and my thoughts are still,
I think about you and know you are ill,
so how can I judge you and leave you alone
for reasons that you know best are set as in stone.
What is truth and what is a lie?
I sit here alone and wonder why
but slowly I turn and walking back
to your side again but one thing I lack;
that I did it not sooner, my arms round you now,
to make your life bearable, the love I can show.

MISSING

The aching inside will not go away,
maybe it's here forever to stay;
maybe to leave me in this state of pain
to soften my heart and give me some gain.
I miss you so much my friend and my love;
I lift up my eyes and looking above,
the vastness of stars fills my empty heart,
the world is so cruel as we play our part
but lifting your eyes the pain now recedes
and lowering again around us there pleads
those that are sick and dying for love
and searching for something that comes from above.

The ache that we feel for those that we miss
can be lost in the fog of that beautiful kiss
of friendship to another whose heart is so sad
and lifts them up to the place that they had
and lost long ago to the pressures of life,
with its sickness and struggles and filled with such strife.

Gently, so gently as hand held in hand,
this was not promised; this was not planned.
Take courage and give it and don't hold it back;
don't feel you cannot or feel that you lack
something to give that is feeling and kind
or not in reality but just in your mind.
That ache that we feel will not go away
but healing will come as for others we stay.

Accepted

Sometimes not accepted by standards of life,
set by others, bringing such strife.
We hang our head and feel empty now
but remember that when we fall and we bow
that all men are equal and must stand alone
and no one has right to lower our tone.

Acceptance is within and not outside;
It is not something for which we run and we hide.
We accept ourselves for just who we are,
what we do in life and just how far
we travel along this dusty path;
some are slow and some are fast.

Accept one another and holding a hand,
as black or white, together we stand,
not judging another for race, culture or creed
or orientation which we do not agree
but accepting our differences, our rights and our wrongs,
then looking above we sing the same song.

Then no one is isolated and standing alone
to live out life's struggle, from the king on the throne
to the poor in the street that sleep in the rain,
suffer in silence, we know not their pain.

Warmth

The warmth of a body that lies next to mine;
the gentle caress in the warm sunshine.
The fondle, the kiss, the beauty we see
in one another as closer we be.

Whatever we are or the hurt that we feel
can be gone in an instant as our love is sealed
with a kiss that is tender but is only a part
of the true love that comes from within the heart.

This love brings warmth and the body will glow,
whether in rain or in cold of snow.
We all have ability to give from within,
do not stifle or this is the sin.

Relax and let ourselves go, lower our pride,
take not for ourselves, in dishonesty hide.
It shows on the face and softens the look;
for all to read, as reading a book.

My Friend

How can you be a friend to me?
When all around: from what I see
reject, disown and turn the back.
They know the difference from white and black,
and live their lives on surface seen
Am I so wrong and hounded so,
with inner struggle and long lost glow;
a world of confusion and despair,
things I find I cannot repair
or change? How can I change myself?
My character, feelings on the shelf?
Be honest, they say and then be free
from guilt and fear and you will see
what it means to live like all of us,
seated on train or car or bus,
and go about your daily life
mechanically so and filled with strife
and pressure, stress until you come
like all of us, under the sun;
then death will claim your useless toil
and you return into the soil.
Majority condemns and strikes the life
that seeks to be different above the strife
but one thing's for sure and you will lend
a helping hand; my one true friend.

Minority

Minority? Culture? Lesbian or gay?
Different to others. Have your say
and do not be afraid to step out of line
to what majority thinks in fixing signs.
All will follow their fellow man,
running, walking, the master plan.
Dare to be alone and standing firm,
although you feel inside, a worm,
worthless, useless in other's eyes.
Be brave, you will increase in size.
Believe what you will and standing strong,
don't run away when you feel wrong.
Face your giant, ignore the pain
and isolation felt and inner strain
as day by day the struggle stays.
No one knows your stumbled ways,
as the world will judge from what they see
with hardness, lack of real pity
and as you stand, feel rain and wind
that beats against you, so unkind;
you will grow stronger, confidence build
and weather-beaten, will not yield.

Aching

Why does the ache that I feel inside
make me want to run and hide?
I tried to find myself and be
exposed to others that I see.
I tried to be honest, then how far

from those I love, I have been barred.
Cannot accept the way I am,
filled with pain and filled with blame.
Unless I choose to be like those,
identity lost, stumble like clones,

tears fall down, hearts that burst;
pain so deep it cannot get worse.

Do we know what isolation feels?
Instead of hurt what ways can heal?
Accepting each other for who we are;
no one rejected and no one barred.

Touch the one who goes astray
with love and acceptance, the only way;
it brings reward, stops pain so deep,
and brings back beauty and peaceful sleep.

Unreachable Love

I see you and watch your lovely ways;
watch what you do to fill your days,
look into your eyes and see the pain,
deep inside I see the stain
of the past you feel; you cannot cry
and release your feelings. You wonder why?
You feel you are of little worth,
feelings that have been since birth.
But you are beautiful to me,
every part of your body.
The parts you hate when you look at yourself.
You have suffered much and not good health.
Others abused you and hurt you deep,
threw you aside into a heap.
My darling you are so special to me,
but I know you can only my dearest friend be,
for another loves you. So silently I bear
what I really feel and how I care
you will never know but be happy my love.
When I see you in his arms, I will back away
and avert my eyes and let you stay.
Inside I feel an ache but yet
something else I know I get.
I smile for you because I know
that you are happy and it shows.

Misunderstanding

What did I say? What did I do?
Do I look for someone new?
Sit in pain and hurt inside;
tears fall down I cannot hide.

Incentive gone to work and clean,
lay in bed and feel so mean.
Search my heart and search my mind;
Is there something there I find?

My love for you was deep inside.
Did you know it? I have not lied.
I miss you so much; why are you hurt?
Why cannot explain? Stuck in the dirt.

I said I was sorry but your pain is the past,
I'd never have hurt you and leave at the last.
I promised to stay and stick to the end;
let me keep that promise my darling friend.

If I could take your hurt away,
and give you back another day.
I would sacrifice my self for you
to enjoy the life that is your due.

Others have hurt you and thrown in the dust,
used and abused you, living their lust;
but all I wanted was to love you right
and see you live; not give up the fight.

Darling I love you, just like my own son,
I care about you as if you're the only one.
I cannot explain my feelings inside,
so strong, now empty; don't turn back the tide.

My love will not die but live to the end
for you, my loyal and faithful friend.
So if I have hurt you and said something wrong,
please understand me; it's for you I long.

I will never leave you, no matter how hard
or rough the passage. Right from the start
I gave you a promise from deep in my heart,
a promise that lasts until we must part.

Inner Feelings

Feelings come and feelings go
but there is one thing that I know,
no matter what you feel inside
there is a door that opens wide.

When you rely upon a fact;
that faith which drives you to an act
will search the wise and deeper thoughts
of knowledge learned by what is taught.

Taught by word and eyes that see
example set by you and me.
A look, a glance, a step away
will show that there's another day.

So look above the feeling, see
the test that comes to you and me.
The mountain seems to dim and fade
and you no longer in the shade.

The sun will shine and seem so bright
the day will come when there was night;
warmth and a smile upon the face,
the step is strong, a quicker pace.

Sacrifice

'Sacrifice', what does it mean?
We know the way forward to work as a team.
We know how to give and share from our heart,
moving together and playing our part.

The books that we read explain how it's done;
to work for each other and bring out the sun.
The kindness we show will reap a reward,
that's not why we do it; in trying to be good.

The proud man, he stands high up on the hill
and shows this to others, in changing their will.
Teachers there are, we know by the score,
pushing us all to try and do more.

Where does it lead us? What does it all cost?
Lay down our lives; give up for the lost.
Others will stare with smile as we give;
the clothes off our backs that others may live.

Secretly proud of all that we do,
all that we say and think that is true.
But what do I spy from the blink of an eye?
A shrivelled old woman, who lay down to die.

She clutched in her hand a bundle of rags,
others walked by in seeing this old hag;
then just now in front of her stood a small child,
looked in her eyes and gave her a smile.

Reached in her rags and pulled out a chain,
with a picture of mother is all that remained
of her squalid possessions, she pressed in the hand
of the child before her was what she had planned.

She remembered that once she was very young,
filled with her laughter and singing her song.
Her own mother died and she fell on hard times,
clothes now all dirty and covered with grime.

Her necklace was precious and all that she had
but giving it now made her heart glad.
At last she had found a friend who would treasure,
the only thing left to her giving her pleasure.

Remember it's not in the rich and the proud
and those who are selfish and rude and loud;
but joy comes from most insignificant things,
that bring their own warmth and make the heart sing.

The Train That Never Comes

Waiting in the station for the train that never comes;
How did I arrive here? Am I the only one?
The aching I feel deep inside; but so deep
that I cannot reach it; only weep.

Torn apart, kicked and bruised.
Am I loved or only used?
Pulled and pushed, this way and that,
Feeling empty and feeling flat.

When the train is here, enough,
if it will carry the one I love.
Often I have waited, if in vain
to find when looking an empty train.

As long as hope is alive in me,
then I will wait and I will see
someone I know step from the train
and waken my heart to beat again.

Do not give up when you wait so long
not in despair; not finding a song;
someone is out there, boarding the train,
searching for you; it is not in vain.

CONFUSION

I open my eyes and what do I see?
A friend who stands there for you and me.
He holds out his hand and beckons me close,
with promises given for better or worse.

He takes my hand in his now and then
I feel so warm and wanted and clean;
My heart feels a glow that spreads through my veins;
at last I can now have a future again.

We go on a trip and see sights so rare,
the fun and the laughter, the hope I did not dare
to imagine, could bring a smile like a beam.
Can this be happening? Or is it a dream?

The life that I lived before was so filled
with pain that affected even my will
to see something positive, something so sweet
that always fell down, smashed at my feet.

Fearful, so fearful that the bubble would burst.
Come on then now and do your worst.
My mind it is racing and tormented inside,
I run and run and try to hide.

From my loneliest place the silence is felt
like a thousand pins, as on the floor I knelt.
Why do I feel this? Not accepting my friend,
the one who came to me, trying to mend.

My heart now is bursting and tears they fall down,
hands that are heavy, head with a frown.
Slowly I lift my eyes and I glance
to my right, in the darkness and there I chance

to see that the one who I had thought gave
up and wandered away with a wave
of his hand in frustration with my obvious pain;
I saw him the one who was there again.

Had knelt by my side and patiently wait,
with hand now in mine; had opened the gate
of floods of the tears that fell to the ground,
as I realised the dream with reality found.

I looked in his face and his eyes were so kind,
melting my coldness and fear that was mine.
Dreams that are nightmares in confusion and pain
can be ignited by love and bring life again.

Wasted Love?

When is love wasted? Or can it be true
that when love is given, it is returned to you.
Just be yourself and if that is your way
to love unconditionally wherever you stray.

Then love is not wasted, if given from heart
that beats with feeling, playing a part
that some cannot find; their door is closed
to love that will change them in highs and the lows.

Giving so much it tears you apart
when your love that is given becomes a dart
returned to you and feeling its pain
will satisfy you when loving again.

Love and pain walk hand in hand
when you give love like grains of sand;
time will tell, so persevere
and spread love around on every tear.

A Beautiful Flower

The sun was shining, with day bright
never was a better sight
as looking in the garden then.
to vibrant, dazzling colour blend.

It pleased the eye, relaxed the mind
and caused the owner to unwind.
Hard work and hands that cut and bruised
were the main tools that he used.

Over painful toil and many tears
to bring to perfection through the years
the plants and flowers that are seen,
red, yellow, blue and green.

One day, the gardener walked the path
of beauty, scent in droplets bathed,
then stopped as gazing down among
the flowers, radiant; a mighty throng.

The sun was shining bright this day
as he carefully wound his way
among his best and brightest blooms;
he chose but one to grace his rooms.

The garden still is clear and bright
but through the window of the night
there is one flower clearly seen
the best and loveliest there has been.

Dedicated to Tanz, January 2009

The Cost

Why don't we sit down and weigh up the cost,
Once we were lonely, once we were lost:
Have we forgotten how it was then
To stumble around in darkness with men
who were selfish and rude, bemoaning their lot,
in terrible panic the fire was so hot
but then a strong hand pulled us out of the fire,
lifting us up and set us much higher.
So what do we owe Him: this person so strong?
who gave us new life and took all our wrong,
He gave up His life for us, what can we give?
When He suffered so much that we all might live.
He sat down alone and counted the cost
to save us, and heal us, the lonely and lost:
so what can I give Him? This is His call
can only respond and give Him my all.

The Mist of Yesterday